Every Fallen Leaf

Every Fallen Leaf

A Book by

Corey McKenna

IngramSpark

La Vergne, Tennessee

Table of Contents

Be Strong and Courageous!
Do not be afraid or
discouraged. For the Lord
your God is with you
wherever you go.

Joshua 1:9

• Introduction •

...in those defining moments

It is in life that our experiences define who we are as individuals. We stop and realize the overarching components in life test our every ability. We cannot begin to describe why it happens that way, but we certainly try to make sense of it. For those who rely on God, his plan for us so much bigger than who we are and, many times, difficult to comprehend how enormous it truly is for us. Throughout our lives, understanding why things happen a certain way can give us a headache. It is in our nature to try and make sense of it, apply it to our lives, understand it, fix it, change it or just plain let it go. It has meaning, however small. It also defines us and what we are capable of accomplishing.

In those moments that defined me, I turn to my own experiences in life that shape me. I find the simplest of things. The basic of things. The myriad of experiences that shape and mold the very essence of who I am. I looked back at the relationships I had in my life – in high school, community college, Fresno State, in other cities. These relationships were instant friends – Jackie Maker, Amanda Morgan, Robin Olson, and Jan Vetter. This friendship was everlasting and helped Jen overcome some of her self-doubts and began to grow and impact so many lives.

The next few years were incredible for Jen, but then her health began its decline. At first, it was the little things, but then the little things got bigger and bigger and more challenging to manage. Breathing became more complicated, and in July 2017, it came to a head in Seward, Alaska. Jen's breathing complications got worse, and she was airlifted to a hospital in Anchorage. As we should have expected, God picked the perfect hospital. The doctor there was a CF specialist and knew Dr. McCarthy quite well. After several days in the hospital, she was released. Still, a month later, a fiery, smoky season in our area caused her to become reliant on oxygen. It was also the point where we decided to attempt the aggressive IV treatment to try and get rid of her bacterial infection.

These were long, difficult, trying days in our lives. Many days required 8+ hours of IV treatment, causing her to be sick, weak, and not do very well. It only got more challenging. The plan was for at least a year, if not longer. Finally, in 2018, we began conversations about a double lung transplant. At first, we had no success. Not one transplant hospital wanted to take her until October 2019. The University of North Carolina, Chapel Hill, called and said they want us to visit. In December 2019, we went for a consultation with no expectation of acceptance. Then, the day before Christmas, our transplant coordinator, Kelly Watson, called us to say they want us to relocate there. What a fantastic Christmas present and a huge answer to years of prayer. In February 2019, we relocated to Chapel Hill and began the lung transplant journey. As we prepared for this move across the country, we had several things to consider: a place to live, a car to drive, extra money, someone to stay with Jen throughout the process. All of this was a huge logistical challenge. Thank goodness I am a planner.

We were blessed by the fantastic people at our church in Coeur d'Alene. A going away and send-off luncheon took place in late January. This was not only a way to say goodbye to us but also to act as a fundraiser. Through the Children's Organ Transplant Association, we raised enough money to stay in North Carolina for several months without adding any significant financial stress to the family. Two of the biggest "stresses" were having a place to live and having a car to drive. Hotels and apartments were out of the question as they were too expensive. We ended up finding a wonderful little home in Pittsboro, NC, about 20 minutes from the hospital. The people who owned it were terrific. One problem solved. Our car problem was also quickly solved. Perry and Anita Safron, friends who lived in the area, purchased a used van for us while staying there. God was good in providing what we needed.

The early months of living in North Carolina were about establishing a routine of doctor visits, physical therapy, more doctor visits, transplant classes, and more doctor visits. As much as possible, I flew back and forth from Idaho to North Carolina, spending time with Jen, learning as much as I could about the transplant process. Finally, on April 5, Jen was placed on the official transplant waiting list. At any moment, a call could come from Kelly that a pair of lungs were available and to get ready.

She was assigned a lung allocation score based on priority level. Her initial score was 43 (out of 100), meaning she was a priority but not that much of a priority. Scores were reevaluated every two weeks and adjusted accordingly. Her scores continued to increase as her condition worsened over April. By the end of April, she was hospitalized. By early May, her score was in the 70s, and by May 15, her score was in the 90s. It was life or death. Then, on May 22, she received a call that a viable pair of new lungs were available. I was on the plane heading on the red-eye to North Carolina. Expecting an 8-10-hour surgery, I was shocked to find that she was already in recovery by the time I landed. I could not get to the hospital fast enough.

Within 24 hours, Jen was sitting up, and the breathing machine was off. She breathed her first full breath of air for the first time without CF-infected lungs. Doctors even got her out of bed and sitting in a chair. Within 36 hours, she was walking a bit. But then, she developed a fever and never truly recovered from it, and her infections got worse. Over the next several weeks, ups and downs ensued but never really amounted to much progress. Doctors tried to figure out things. We were so very fortunate to have them in our corner. Near the end, I will never forget the moment the two surgeons came out of her room with that look of despair, sadness, and defeat, telling me I need to call the families to come out to North Carolina. There was nothing they could do. Further surgery would result in additional complications and even death on the operating table. Her body had finally given up, and God had called her home to heaven. I just broke down. The most challenging thing I have ever had to do was tell Jen the doctors could not fix her. Tears began to stream down her face. She knew.

When Jen decided to write a book back in early 2019, it was such a great idea because she would articulate all of the things that many of us did not know or understand. But, after her passing, those thoughts never came about, so I decided to make it happen for her. While I could not quite articulate them perfectly, nor was I able to capture everything, I decided to ask several people in her life if they would be willing to write a chapter. Of course, several asked, "What do I write about?" I said, "whatever you want and however God speaks to your heart. It will all work out just fine." Now, I asked many people and was a little surprised some said no while others jumped at the chance to put something on paper. To that end, these upcoming chapters come from the heart of those who were influenced by her, captured by her love and disposition, and enamored by how she battled through some challenging moments.

So, why the title *Every Fallen Leaf*? It is a metaphor for life. We are naturally afraid of change, afraid to commit, afraid to leap. Many run away, chasing leaves falling from a tree, ready to be swept off their feet, overcoming the difficulty of giving oneself entirely to another person. It is being afraid to let go. It is about having faith in what could be, not what the world consistently negates, that life will move forward, no matter what. There is hardship, and there is a struggle. And no matter how much you want peace, life will always throw you curveballs. It is about the strength and courage that Jen exhibited throughout this journey.

Jen was the very definition of strength and courage. She fit all of these characteristics. She went into this whole thing with vim and vigor, with eyes focused on what God had planned. For years, we prayed for a cure. While the cure for CF was "not going to happen," it was the tenaciousness of her doctors to find ways to get her what she needed. We know God put those individuals in our path, and it was Him who made that possible. But it was Jen who took things and never lost hope. She was determined to see it through, no matter how bad she felt from all the medication. She changed the landscape of what it meant to be entirely reliant on God. It was like chasing every fallen leaf in the breeze. It was in those defining moments we saw the impact she had on all of us. This book shares that and is dedicated to everyone who contributed to it.

· *One* ·

Every Fallen Leaf on the Breeze

Corey McKenna

Moments in life take time to develop, grow, and become what they are for each of us. Our relationships, romantic or otherwise, develop, and we figure out whether it is worth taking it to the next level. Over time, we find ourselves smitten by a significant other, to the point it becomes much more than just friends. It may start as a date. You find out if each person is compatible with the other. Sometimes it works out, and other times it does not. Sometimes it takes time to know if it works out or not. Maybe years. Two individuals may realize it is not worth it, and they go their separate ways. However, there are times when two individuals know immediately they are compatible and want to pursue a deeper, more meaningful relationship with one another. Togetherness. We took care of each other over the years. Every day brought opportunities to grow as a couple. We did wear our hearts on our sleeves because we were sensitive to each other's needs. In relationships, people give their hearts to each other as a sign of trust and devotion. We were no different. That magic marker made it permanent, and the world could not wash it away – ever.

Jen and I found each other in a class at National University in Bakersfield, California, in early 2002. She was a student in one of the courses I was teaching at the university. I know what you are thinking, and no, we did not date while she was in my class. We barely spoke to each other. She took courses from me during that year, but it was not until a year later that we met up again. I was coming to teach a new course, and she was waiting out at her truck for a friend to finish one. We got to talking. The next thing I know, Jen asks me if I would like to go shooting and a milkshake afterward. "Was she asking me out on a date?" I thought. Maybe she was. Never having shot a gun before, I said, "Sure. Let's go." I think she was a little taken back by my okay.

What could have been better than guns and a milkshake afterward? Little did either of us know it was to blossom into something more. Both of us were coming off relationships that were going nowhere or were just plain rough. We just found each other at that right moment. In some way, we both just knew, even though it was still in its "getting-to-know-you" phase. When we had the opportunity to go on an official date, I planned something she would never forget – we went flying. I booked a private plane, went to the airport, and flew around Bakersfield. Granted, we had a pilot with us, but he did let Jen fly for a bit. Afterward, we had dinner at the house.

Over the coming months, we continued to learn more about each other, as any new couple would, I suppose. We were officially a couple in September 2003. After that first "official" date, we went to Magic Mountain amusement park and then saw the opening of *Kill Bill Volume 1*. Not surprisingly, she liked roller coasters and Quentin Tarantino movies. Together we started going to Laurelglen Bible Church in Bakersfield. We did the *40 days of Purpose* together. For the first time, I met Galen and Lita Norsworthy, who were pastors of the college group at LBC and are here today. Galen ultimately married us on Jan 1, 2005, in a tiny chapel on the coast in Cambria, CA. And over time, we worked through the ups and downs of her CF by making quarterly trips to LA to visit her CF doctors. It was what we did. She loved her TV shows: *Andy Griffith, Cheers, Frazier, Justified, Big Bang Theory, MASH,* and countless others. But our absolute favorite: *Seinfeld*. Everything we learned, we learned from *Seinfeld*. It was another Festivus miracle. We had a cute puppy dog, Pudge, and for a while, three Siamese kitties — Claudia, Aja, and Ra. Our little home, with fur babies, kept us going every day.

Jen got me back doing triathlons. Triathlon was in my blood. I had been involved in the sport since I was 16 years old. I got to tackle my first Ironman in Arizona in 2006. Since then, I have completed 14 Ironman-distance triathlons and numerous others with her as my biggest fan. Many of them were with our amazing friends from Bakersfield – Josh and Katie Lewis.

I love that Ironman is challenging. It requires serious discipline, commitment, time, and effort. It is not something an athlete takes·lightly, nor does he or she decide one day I want to do this without having an established background. Fueled by the desire to prove myself in difficult athletic events, Ironman-distance triathlons push me to the brink — harsh conditions, challenging courses, and mental fatigue. Depending on where one competes dictates the course and the challenges the area brings. It reminded me of how hard it was for her every day.

She was always my cheerleader for these events. She would travel with me to various locations to be my support. If it was an Ironman event, spectators have an extremely long day, just as long as the athletes. It is a lot of just sitting around watching unknown athletes go by on the bike and run. Sometimes, it could be three hours or longer before a spectator sees his or her athlete. Some venues are not spectator-friendly, whereas others provide multiple opportunities. Shorter triathlons are much better for spectators and provide many vantage points for them to see athletes. After many Ironman events, it was time for me to venture out into a different kind of triathlon.

In July 2017, I committed to a new kind of racing experience — one called extreme triathlon as if Ironman wasn't hard enough. It's more challenging than an Ironman in that you are required to bring your support crew who are committed to getting you across that finish line. My first Xtri — Alaskaman Extreme Triathlon - was a 2.6-mile cold glacier water swim in Resurrection Bay, a 113-mile bike along the Seward Highway that contained strong headwinds and 5000 feet of climbing. The race ended with a 27-mile run with nearly 10,000 feet of climbing that included two mountain climbs. It is plain difficult, and yes, Ironman is hard enough already, but this takes it to the next level. Alaskaman, like many extreme triathlons, provided some unique challenges. An athlete had to provide his or her equipment and nutrition. This was also a self-supported event.

Along with my support crew, we traveled to Alaska in July of 2017 and checked into the event. It was exciting. The vibe was different than Ironman events. It was low-key. After check-in, we all went to lunch to relax. That's when things changed when life said, "not so fast." The race experience turned into a life-or-death experience. Jen started suffering from breathing complications and needed to be airlifted from our tiny little town in the southern part of Alaska to a hospital in Anchorage. I immediately dropped out of the race. There was no, let's wait and see, not thinking it about or discussing with my support crew. I knew my decision immediately. Jen broke into tears when I told her that I was dropping out. I looked at her and said, "honey, it is just a race, and it will be here next year." I was committed to making sure that she was okay. So, they airlifted her to a hospital in Anchorage and drove there in the middle of the night. For the time being, she was okay. I went back to Seward the next day to pick up my support team.

She stayed in the hospital for several days before she was released. The hospital gave her an O_2 concentrator for the plane. That proved challenging, but we made it home after spending an extra week in Anchorage. We ended up going back in July 2018 to complete the race with Jen and my support crew. They did get me across the finish line. Throughout the race, Jen had to have her IV meds with her the whole time. She was a trooper through it all. However, our life experiences were about to take a different turn a month later. Jen became reliant on oxygen, and her cystic fibrosis got progressively worse. We had a difficult road ahead, to make difficult decisions, to travel a road that will test who we were as a married couple.

Like every fallen leaf on the breeze, we are destined to end up somewhere. I believe leaves symbolize what I think God wants to accomplish in our lives. I believe we were destined to be in North Carolina for that double lung transplant. We were also supposed to come back from North Carolina together, but it did not happen that way. It was not what I expected, but maybe this was God's plan all along. Over time, I reflected on the why. Why did this happen? Why did the excitement turn to tragedy? Why did God let us go all this way only to have her die? Why is God punishing me? No question, I was mad at God. I did not know which direction to go. Darkness persisted for a long time; it continues even today as I discover new dimensions of that loss. I think, in some ways, she let me off the hook, permitting me to let go. I worked hard to keep her well, to keep her safe, to protect her, to do anything for her – all those years. Though I experienced death, I also experienced life in ways I never thought possible before – not after the darkness, as we might suppose, but in the darkness. I did not go through the pain and come out the other side; instead, I lived in it and found the grace to survive and eventually grow within the pain. I did not get over my wife's loss; instead, I absorbed the loss into my life, like soil receives decaying matter until it became part of who I am. Sorrow took up permanent residence in my soul and enlarged it. I learned over time that the deeper we plunge into suffering, the deeper we can enter a new and different life – a life no worse than before and most likely better.

I would lie awake in the dark, tormented by the loss. I was emotionally drained all day. I even stopped going to church for a while because I was tired of people asking me all the time how I was doing. I know they meant well. I probably exacerbated the problem by telling people virtually nothing about my struggles. Friends and family marveled at how well I was doing. But inside, I was dying. There were moments where I felt the abyss of emptiness, not to the point of despair or hopelessness, but one where my best friend, my love, my wife was gone.

Every person experiences loss. Loss is a solitary experience. It is unique within ourselves, and when someone says, "you have no idea what I have gone through and how much I have suffered," they are exactly correct. I would even tell people to quit telling me how to grieve or for how long. None of us have any way of knowing what the other person experienced. Each person's experience is his or her own, even if, on the surface, the experience looks the same. How we respond to loss makes each person's experience different from all others. God provides comfort in the most difficult and challenging times; even we are in that darkness, that solitary loneliness.

Eventually, my confidence in God had become quieter but oddly stronger. I was still mad, do not get me wrong, but I think it drew me closer. I felt little pressure to impress Him or prove myself, yet I wanted to find ways to serve Him. I slowly learned where God belonged in my life and how He fit in it. I found solace in knowing there was purpose in Jen's death, that He had a purpose for it, that her work physically on earth was complete, and that she is no longer struggling or in pain. That brought a sense of peace in me. I also learned that life was way too short to deal with people's nonsense. It changed perspectives on life, making me realize it was time to make adjustments, to not put up with the self-perpetuating pettiness of people and to find a better place. I was ready to move forward, little by little, one foot in front of the other, wherever the wind took me.

· Two ·

A Joy Harvested

Katie Lewis

Friends know one of my favorite things to write in a birthday card is "I am so glad that the Good Lord saw fit to have us walk this great earth at the same time and in the same place."

I get the privilege of sharing a few pages of Jen's story because God, in His grace, made her part of my story. As with any story, I think it best to simply start from the beginning . . . well, maybe a quick prologue (it won't surprise many to read that Ironman triathlon training was involved). My husband, Josh, had a new and budding friendship with a guy he'd met at the pool. He and his new pal, Corey, decided in between laps that the husbands and the wives should all get together because we'd surely be fast friends. And so, a plan was made, and dates were set, before I could decide how I felt about it one way or another. Truth be told, I was a bit skeptical and had no notion that I *needed* to be friends with Jen and Corey McKenna. The next thing I knew, I was knocking on their door to share a crockpot dinner. Jen (a small yet mighty gal) answered the door with one hand on the collar of a Golden Retriever–Chow Mix, who was jumping at her side like she was playing with a giant furry yo-yo. I can close my eyes and see this moment playing like a movie in my head. Jen was holding on for dear life to this bouncing flop-eared, tongue-flapping dog with one hand and welcoming us in with the other. Jen's giggles folded into uncontrollable laughter and then . . . a snort laugh exploded out. (You know the kind I'm talking about—the snort that gets everyone laughing even when they don't want to.) And that was it. It happened in the blink of an eye just as Jen shrugged, "Well, I guess now we *have* to be friends because you've heard my snort laugh."

Isn't that the truth for so many of us? A stranger becomes a friend in a moment of laughter. For friends of Jen, this is especially true. The woman loved to laugh and knew how to laugh out loud. I think subconsciously a lot of us spent a good amount of energy trying to make Jen laugh because she was so fun to laugh *with*. My husband, Josh, has done some pretty crazy things to make Jen bust a gut. Buttons flying. Daikon shenanigans. Pun after pun after pun was relentlessly thrown at us. Even when we had to wait a few minutes for Jen to catch her breath and cough her way out of a laughing fit, her huge smile was contagious. The part we didn't talk about for a long time and most people (strangers and friends alike) didn't want to face was that Jen suffered each moment with the reality of Cystic Fibrosis. Those belly laughs and snort laughs were almost always riddled with coughing fits because Cystic Fibrosis is in every breath of a patient's life.

The time our friendship launched was a season of relatively stable health for Jen; Corey and Jen and Josh and I got to make countless more memories together in the simple things—dinner (salted caramel ice cream) and lots and lots of laughter (sometimes even a good snort laugh). The fur-babies even became fast friends. I didn't know it at the time, but Jen was teaching me volumes about one of the most profound mysteries of this life: Suffering and joy are inexplicably bound together. She knew when she woke up, "This is the day that the Lord hath made, I will rejoice and be glad in it." She understood this on a level that was woven into everyday life—even when she didn't feel it, even when she was fiercely depressed, she KNEW it. I will never forget one of our first trips to Coeur D'Alene (after their move). Jen was fighting an infection and was doing some extra IV meds, which meant extra time in "her chair," but she was so excited to take us California kids to Cabella's to check out all of the toys. (If you don't know Cabella's, think Walmart for outdoor adventures.) I insisted I didn't mind hanging at home with her. She insisted she didn't want to miss out. So, she hung her IV from the coat hook in the backseat of the rental car, and off we went. Well, the IV bag wasn't empty when we got to Cabella's, but Jen didn't want to miss an opportunity to give a tour through the store. That crazy woman hopped out of the car and carried her IV bag through the store laughing and smiling all the while. No doubt a few workers and customers went home that day and told their families about "IV girl" but my Dad (who was traveling with us) said she would forever hold the title of "amazing" after witnessing her determination. That was just it: In her actions, she was saying to the wide world, "This is the day."

As things with Team McKenna began to ramp up and fundraising was in full force, it was so fun to hear people's stories about Jen; most had no idea she managed Cystic Fibrosis and those who did had no idea the severity. My friends who got to meet her just once or twice were truly floored by the knowledge of her illness and impending lung-transplant. I have to laugh that to those who met her at my baby shower, I never knew she lived in their memories as "knife-girl" because she came to my rescue as I struggled to open a gift that was tied with some kind of unbreakable elfin thread. I was struggling...pulling, pulling, trying to untie, and pulling again...and Jen yelled out, "OH! I can help!" and whipped out her jumbo pocketknife.

Jen was never a CF girl or transplant girl. She was a giggling girl, an amazing girl, a knife girl. She was something much more than even the sum of her parts. She was Jen. It is some kind of riddle the greatest philosophers of any age would struggle to unravel. Did Jen's suffering amplify her joy in this life? Or did her joy mitigate her suffering? Don't misunderstand. Jen didn't walk around with a fake smile plastered on her face (although so many people had a day in their story marked by the gift of her great, big, smile). Jen lived in reality and her reality was often painful. Hours spent managing (or mismanaging) home treatments every day. Her port-a-cath had to be flushed and cleaned, veins blown during IV treatments. The ongoing battle with food and digestion for someone who loved to eat more than anyone I've ever known. For Jen's sake, I must take an aside and ask everyone reading to appreciate the miracle that is high-quality bacon. But really, if you haven't had a good piece of bacon recently, Jen would want you to address this issue as soon as possible. Lucky for you, it makes pretty much everything better.

Ok, now that we have shared a laugh and we are beginning to be friends, I can stop with the ponderings and give it to you straight. This is the heart of it all . . . Jen's joy was cultivated. She did the hard work of tending the soil of her heart and planting seeds of truth. Jen (with God's help) did the most painful work of pulling out the weeds of self-loathing, which threatened to choke out the blossoming freedom of self-acceptance. Jen knew that she was loved by a benevolent Creator. Jen knew that she was called to love others in His name. Jen knew she must show up with the gifts that were uniquely hers. Jen trusted that when she didn't have what was needed in a moment, Christ would fill in the gaps with miracles. Jen knew that prayer was a powerful place to start. Jen knew that scripture was a dependable anchor. The disciplines of study, prayer, and fellowship grew so much peace, joy, and contentment in Jen's life, it was disarming. She, quite literally, became a friend to the friendless in many cases. Her service to addicts in recovery and their families was priceless. I will confess that I had to fight my tendency to be envious of the time Jen's CDA "tribe" of girlfriends got to share with her. At the same time, I got the blessing of watching my friend move into a chapter of freedom and service in her church community that I still wonder at. Thank you, God, for calling Corey and Jen to CDA during the last years of her life so that she was able to live her last years in full color and full bloom.

After Jen's passing, I spent a lot of time and energy trying to make sense of it. In reality, my heart and mind are still wandering in and out of acceptance and disbelief daily. I have 4 beautiful children under the age of 8 in my house, which means every single moment of my day is the sacred mundane. And, so I play peek-a-boo while mourning, I wash and fold diapers while grieving. I scramble eggs while crying. As a home-schooling family, I am constantly learning when I think I am teaching. A "Jen moment" surprised me shortly after her passing. I was reading aloud to my kiddos from a short story about a kind-hearted Robin whose cheerful song annoys the more pessimistic woodland creatures. The Robin's gladsome spirit starts to grate when the reality of winter sets in but, "It is easy to boast while the sun still shines, if ever so little; but it is not till the storm comes, that the mettle of principle is known." When I read that line aloud to my kiddos it all became crystal clear; Jen's joy was cultivated like the Robin's. She knew where to find nourishment in the dark and cold seasons of her heart. She studied the Bible. She prayed. She wove herself into her community. She laughed—a lot.

One of my last golden memories with Jen was on a trip to Alaska. This was a season of serious health decline, and we all knew a double lung transplant was the only next step in her medical treatment. Jen was only able to walk about 10 yards without assistance and was on oxygen almost constantly. It was the first time it seemed people saw her condition before they saw her. There were sideways glances as she was wheeled through the airport, inquiring looks as she put on her face mask, sympathetic stares as she lost and then caught her breath trying to order a meal. For me, a shift took place when we were hanging out at our vacation rental in Seward, chit-chatting and laughing. I was entertaining her with some recent shenanigans of my three little stooges (I mean boys). Jen started in with her signature laugh but the laugh didn't roll into a snort. This time it evolved into a violent coughing fit which went on for what felt like minutes and culminated when she (quite literally) hacked up a bloody-green-gooey mess from her lungs. The gravity of the moment wasn't lost on either of us. In the silence that followed her coughing fit, I realized that while Jen was coughing nonstop, I'd been apologizing nonstop. I added one last, "I'm sorry," for good measure. Jen looked me full in the face with an ear-to-ear grin and replied, "Don't be. The laugh was worth it."

Now, as I write these words, we are living a part of her story none of us had written. Thanksgiving came and went. Her Birthday came and went. Christmas came and went. We are looking ahead to a new year *without* her walking around on God's green earth at the same time and in the same place. We are here and she is not. I know I had written another chapter...one with hikes, fishing, cruises, and dinners that should be called feasts. Instead, we are here separated by death and facing the unimaginable. My story goes on without her. It is tempting to let my imagination run wild and envision what Jen is doing now. I can see her sprinting around the backyard, wrestling the ball out of the new furbabies' mouths, free and strong...I see her as a space cowgirl, captain of a ship (with Corey as her co-pilot, of course), smiling as she swaps tales with ruffians at a sky café about how many zombie aliens she took out in her last intergalactic shoot-out. There would be throwing stars and knife fights. She'd have a cool wound she could show off. But then I hear Jen, in her kind but firm voice, saying...

"Aw, that story was awesome. I like the shotgun you picked for me."

(We'd laugh...yes, it is a snorting laugh.)

We'd sit quietly for a moment.

She'd let me cry.

And then she'd let me make up a cool named for her Space Mini, and we'd giggle some more.

After a few moments, she'd place her hand lovingly on my arm and say,

"But, Katie, we don't have to make this story up. The Good Lord told us this part of the story. We don't have to imagine it. He has taken the sting from death. He welcomed me into His house and greeted me with open arms as His Good and Faithful servant. I am healed. I am sitting at the table He prepared for me, and it is a feast. I have joined the company of heaven and I pray:

'I pray that Christ may live in your hearts by faith,

I pray that you will be filled with love,

I pray that you will be able to understand how wide, how long, how high, and how deep his love is.'" —Galatians 3:17-18

• *Three* •

Are There Fireflies in Heaven?

Virginia Williams

As Jen's mother, I guess you can say I'm the one who knew her the longest. She always had a sweet, tender nature, even while in the womb. I could feel just gentle, polite taps as if to be asking, "May I come out now?" No big sweeping movements like her brother did. Her father was never able to feel Jen's movements. However, Joe's in utero movements could be seen from across the room. It was as though he was stretching his leg, moving them from one side of my tummy to the other. She came into our lives at 7 pounds 8 ounces and 16 inches. She and her brother looked so much alike when babies that I often needed to look at their clothes to know which was which.

We were fortunate to have a pediatrician, Dr. Goldman, who had interned in the Cystic Fibrosis Department at Children's Hospital – Oakland. The things you learn when things aren't quite right. During the first two weeks after birth, all babies lose some birth weight and, if all goes well, gain their birth weight back. Jen did not. She was just a few ounces shy of her birth weight. After about 5 or 6 weeks of weekly weight checks, we went to Modesto for a sweat test.

CF patients excrete excess salt in their sweat. Try getting a 3-month-old baby to sweat in early March! We found a warm wall and held her up against the wall. The test proved positive. (Too much sodium chloride.) Hard to believe such a simple test can indicate such a diagnosis. We were then referred to Children's Hospital in Oakland, California, to confirm the test since they had an entire CF Department with doctors specializing in CF. It, too, was positive for CF.

Within a month, I learned that when you can see the base of a baby's neck sucking in, it can mean they have pneumonia. The doctor called Children's Hospital and said we would be there that night. Since her father was working and unable to make the trip with me, I called my mother, and we took Jen to Oakland Children's Hospital.

I don't remember what time we arrived, but it was late at night. It was there that I learned how to treat Jen with percussion therapy, how to suction phlegm from hopefully her lungs, put her in a tent, and lose her in the fog of fine mist in hopes of hydrating her airway and make the mucous in her lungs thinner. Mind you, I never thought I would torture my child by making her gag several times each treatment. But, if it meant her life, then you will quickly learn you must. It wasn't pretty, but I had to do it if I wanted to keep her alive. If my memory serves me, there are 21 different areas where I would pat her firmly with a cupped hand, rolling her sideways and upside down for the different lobes suctioning her airway each time I changed her position. I should explain that this suctioning wasn't pleasant. It would require pushing a tube up her nose and down her airway, down to her lungs, all the while gagging her. The daily process took about 30 minutes. Not all of it was bad. She loved the percussion portion, but as soon as she heard the Gomco (suction machine), she'd let me know she didn't like that part. She'd push away from me and voiced her opinion on the matter.

Her brother was none too pleased with me at first. I was hurting his sister! After all, Jen was *his* sister! He loved her and was a protective big brother. After a few explanations, it soon became a daily routine that he accepted. Like his father, he was quiet, observant, and protective of Jen. You knew how seriously he took being her big brother when we were at the doctor's office getting the usual immunization shots. I was standing holding Jen while Joe stood next to me, carefully watching the nurse Jen her shot in her thigh. When she began to cry, he began to cry and let me know I failed. Boy! Was I in trouble!

But, like most siblings, he would tease her – a lot. I will say, like father, like son. This was part of her learning to be tougher than she already was. She took every joke and teased in great stride and would give it back to them. She was never a wimp, and she knew all of it was with love. The best part was that somehow, we all just instinctively let Jen be Jen. We never told her she couldn't do something because of her CF. In retrospect, she would have just tried harder to prove she could.

I would be remiss in not telling you about a blessing in disguise – well, not in disguise but not understood at the time. My children were being watched by a lovely Christian lady who said something to me that God had tucked away in my memory bank. When we first learned of Jen's diagnosis, Anita Wilson told me we were blessed because God chose Jen for a special purpose. Mind you, I couldn't see the blessing at the time. I felt myself tense up and wasn't being very Christian in my thoughts! Surprisingly, nothing came out of my mouth chastising her for not understanding what our future was going to be. However, Anita was exactly right! Talk about God being in control!

My relationship with the Lord was minimal at best, but I learned to pray fervently for Jen. I even did that parent thing and asked God to give me CF and free Jen of the daily treatments and give her an entire life free of CF. Well, I didn't get the CF, but I never had to make her gag after she was 11 months old. Since her father was a police officer working the graveyard shift, I was home alone with both my children. Around 2 a.m., I woke up, my room was aglow, and I heard a voice telling me not to worry and that "Jen will be fine." Hearing the Lord tell you something is different than hearing someone talk to you. I can't explain it, but it's different.

Now I ask you if you heard an unfamiliar voice talking to you in the middle of the night, wouldn't you be alarmed, get your gun out, run to the children's room and call the police? Nope. I went back to sleep! That morning, I thought I dreamt it all. However, her treatment was the 1st thing I did. Hallelujah!!!

It wasn't a dream! You see, usually, when I used the GOMCO (suction device), her phlegm was so thick that I needed to follow by sucking water through the clear plastic tube. That morning, her phlegm was much thinner! To give you an example of the difference, think of when you have a horrible chest cold and cough and cough only to struggle to move that awful thick gunk in your lungs and esophagus. Compare that with your everyday mucous or sputum. That was the difference between night and day. I didn't dream it! It wasn't until later did I realize the glow in my room that night was the glow of God's presence.

Jen was never fully cured of CF, but I never had to push the tube down her throat ever again. She was able to live about as normal a life as one could expect. She did still need her enzymes to help her digest her foods. We did continue to have regular checkups with her CF physician.

Like all children, Jen wanted to be "normal" like all her friends. The only reason her schoolmates knew there was a problem was that she had to go to the office to take her enzymes for her meals. The enzymes helped her to digest her food. An explanation for enzymes follows. She was not allowed to keep it on her and take it on her own. This drew attention to her, and she didn't like it. Nope, not at all. This did become a problem because she decided not to take her enzymes at lunch instead of making it obvious. Why enzymes?

Cystic fibrosis is a misnomer. The thick mucus tends to clog the pancreas, which secretes enzymes to help digest your food. It not only obstructs the pancreas but also minimizes the absorption surface in the intestines. That's why she could eat so much and not gain weight! Anyway, she was supposed to take enzyme capsules with her meals to help digest her food.

On the outside, she was a compliant child but, on the inside, she quietly rebelled. You've heard that little story about the little boy who was commanded to sit. When he sat, he said he might be sitting down physically, but, in his heart, he was standing.

Well, that was Jen. She never talked back to me nor argued with me. If I ever had to "talk with her" (usually about taking care of her health), she would just look at me with those big brown eyes and never say a word. So, parents out there that have an argumentative child, be thankful.

From the time she could walk, she had her ideas of what clothes she would wear and what she would do. Even as a toddler, I would dress her in cute girly clothes, and she would go back to her room, pull out the clothes she liked and would change her clothes – usually a T-Shirt and pants. No frilly girly clothes for her!

In her high school years, she was determined to prove she was "normal." Instead of getting her full 8 hours of sleep each night as advised by her doctor, she would pull all-nighters with homework and then proceed to school. Once, when she had a mild case of pneumonia, she went to school anyway. No, I wasn't able to make her stay home. Since she was in high school, I felt that she would soon be leaving home and that she had to take responsibility for her health.

If she failed, she failed while she still lived at home, and I would be there. She did just fine with her mild pneumonia and never missed a day of school because of it. Her pneumonia was not because she caught a cold. You see, secondary cigarette smoke was the reason she would get bronchitis which developed into pneumonia. Once we realized that, her family and friends who did smoke wouldn't smoke near her again.

Soon, she was of age to drive. Like most young people with a "condition" who live in denial, she wasn't making the best choices. I even tried to leverage it with her getting her driver's license. If she couldn't make good decisions on a long-term basis, how could I trust that she could exhibit good judgment in an instant when driving? Well, more for need rather than anything else, she finally got her license, and she proved me wrong. She was a good driver and exhibited wise judgment.

Since her father and I had divorced, she would drive to Sonora, California, to visit her father. This was a 240-mile drive from Bakersfield to Sonora. To add to her mother's concern, she didn't go up Highway 99 to Modesto and stay on the major highways. She would take the backcountry roads leaving Highway 99 at Merced. A mother must tell her child to be careful. Well, as a dutiful mother, as she got into her car, I said, "Be careful." She stopped, turned and looked at me, and said, "And you think I won't?" I chuckled because I knew she would. It was then that I explained to her that it was my job and duty as a mother to tell her that because if something did happen to her, it would be my fault. She grinned because she understood me.

From that day forward, if I ever felt the need to be a dutiful mother, we'd look at each other and say, "It's a mom thing." She never objected to it. She knew I **HAD** to say it and would smile, and sometimes we'd both chime in, saying, "It's a Mom thing."

I want to add a little note here that her father and I made a point of never making Jen feel nor think she was disabled. She was able to do or try anything she wanted and try she did. She never considered herself handicapped. I believe she always wanted to prove she wasn't. Even when she could have stayed home because she pulled an all-nighter for school homework, she wouldn't stay home. I couldn't get her to stay home.

There was a short period in her teens where she was not taking care of herself. I tried to talk with her several times about how she must take care of herself and do as the doctor ordered. Finally, in tears, I begged her to take care of herself and asked her why she felt she didn't need to. It was then that she told me because she didn't know how long she would live. I was shocked since I know she knew what God had told me and that I fully expected she would live a full life. Because of an unfortunate circumstance, she felt I was hiding something about her health and had not been honest with her. After I told her I had always been honest with her, we never had to have the talk again. She realized I had been honest with her, and she started being more responsible for her health.

When she was in college, she started showing signs of lung deterioration. On rare occasions, she would begin to bleed in her lungs. She could feel it and would cough up blood. This was after she had contracted an infection that the doctors could not get rid of it. Perhaps it would be better understood if I explain how the deterioration of the lungs happens.

I read an article while waiting for her doctor's appointment at the CF clinic. Her lungs' mucous is so thick that the harmful bacteria become enveloped by her thick mucus, which becomes a protective wall. When the white blood cells detect the bacteria, it starts oozing enzymes to kill the bacteria but to no avail. Because the white blood cells keep trying to kill the bacteria, the enzyme begins to dissolve or eat away the lung tissues, losing the precious alveoli or air sacs in the lungs.

She was an excellent employee. The employers she had loved her and were glad to have her work for them. The job she enjoyed the most was in a sporting and gun shop – Second Amendment Sports. There, she became an assistant manager. This little 5'3" gal learned self-defense, judo, and anything and everything about guns, rifles, shotguns. She could tell you what load would go, how far, the velocity, and how effective it was around. I think it was a good thing they didn't carry bazookas and canons! She could even teach people how to shoot a bow and arrow because she became an excellent archer.

Now that I think about it, I chuckle, considering how she was surprised I could hit a target. I'm not sure why she thought I hadn't shot a handgun before. Her father was the range master for the Sonora Police Department. He took me to the shooting range several times and taught me to shoot and hit a target.

Although she never told me, I'm pretty sure Duane had taken Jen to the firing range and taught her some things too. He was quite the marksman. I even saw him hit his target when shooting from the hip old West style! Archery. As a teen, she decided to take up archery.

She found a store where she could use their equipment to shoot and had a few archery groups. She joined the Junior Olympic Archery Development (JOAD) program and became quite the archer. For about 4 or 5 years, we would go to tournaments. She placed in a couple but had more fun trying. I like the fact that she was competitive and a good sport. Winning wasn't everything for her. As long as she did her best, she was happy. We were grateful to my then-husband because it became rather expensive, and he supported her 100%.

Besides the week she spent at four months old, she had never been admitted to the hospital for pneumonia. She had a strong immune system and a stronger mind. At the time she was diagnosed, the doctors told us that the life expectancy of CF patients is in the mid-20s

God not only blessed us by answering my prayers but blessed us abundantly. She lived twice as long as expected. Yes, there are many types of CF, some much milder and some much worse. Jen had the common one. We were blessed to have her for 41 years and seven months.

She developed a deep love for God and helped me realize how much more I needed God and to love God more. When she was seven years old, while driving to church, she told me her little friend told her she knew all about Jen's condition. When I asked her what h she said, she said her friend told her she would die. Well, you can imagine how I felt! What nerve!

How dare she tell Jen she was going to die! Why that impudent little child! I swear, I could have bent the steering wheel. Again, God stepped in, and I heard this calm, sweet voice coming out of me asking Jen, "What do you think of that?" Jen replied, "I know Jesus is taking care of me." Her faith was already strong. This wasn't the first time she learned that CF people die.

A few months later, a true movie told the story of a young girl with CF who died at a very young age. When I realized which movie it was, I would change it, but she already knew what it was all about and wanted to watch it. After the movie was over, I asked her what she thought. You're right. She knew Jesus was taking care of her. I'd like to explain that the Lord had always had His hand on both of us.

He kept me from reacting in such a way that Jen would be alarmed about her condition. She never thought of herself as handicapped for any reason at all. Why she even tried to join the Navy to become an airplane mechanic. You guessed it. She was not recruited. Boy, was she unhappy about that!

As Jen matured, what surprised me was how open she had become. She was honest and trustworthy. What you saw was the true Jen. She made herself vulnerable to reach out to those who needed someone to confide in, share problems with, and share with Jesus.

The last four months with Jen were a sweet privilege. She was so brave and cared more about others. Her concern for me after losing my husband just before going to North Carolina gave me strength. We didn't talk about it, but her mere presence and calm nature were all I needed. My daughter was fine and was going to enjoy life with lungs not riddled with CF.

Jen was strong in faith, and it showed. She was also mentally the strongest person I know. I've always said that if her body was as strong as her mind, there would be no stopping her and that she would be with us now instead of enjoying life in heaven with Jesus.

One day in April 2019, before her transplant, Jen's need for increased O₂ was increasing. To my surprise, she told me she felt she was dying. To this day, I'm not sure why I wasn't more reassuring because I had always felt and believed that God was giving me peace because He was going to bring her through the transplant and that we would all return to Coeur d'Alene celebrating a successful transplant. Anyway, instead of reassuring her that she would live, I assured her that a heaven is a beautiful place and that Steve has no desire to leave heaven. That had to be another time when God intervened and had a message for Jen.

After Jen's surgery, she was limited in what she could do. Using the call button you commonly see in hospital beds was too much for her. As a result, I would hold her hands through the night to squeeze them if she needed me. Because I stayed with her 24/7 and a full night's sleep is an unknown there, I was more exhausted than I realized. One night, I guess I had reached my limit, and she was unable to wake me. The nurses rolled my recliner away from her bed, did their routine checks, bathed her, the x-ray tech took her daily x-ray, then moved me back. I slept through it all. I had asked her BFF Jackie Sisco-Maker to bring a small bell to tie on her fingers so she could ring for me if I weren't near her. Well, the bell didn't wake me that night. Jen, in all her humor, let me know the bell system was flawed. She tossed it aside, never to be used again. Jackie and I still laugh at Jen's show of humor and expression over this. I continued to hold her hand every night Corey wasn't there. I was so privileged!

How do I personally handle the loss of my husband and daughter within a few months of each other? God. Yes, without God, I hate to think what my state of mind would be. He has provided a wonderful family who loves and cares for me. I've also been "adopted" by Jen's BFF Jackie Sisco-Maker and her husband, Mike. They are always there to ensure I'm doing well – primarily through the holiday season and the anniversary of Steve's passing. But on my alone times, I don't look at what I no longer have, but focus on all the beautiful blessings and memories God gives me - blessings not only about Jen and Steve but what He has done to comfort me through this last year and continues to bless me with even today. No words can express my gratitude to God for carrying me so close to Him.

Lastly, she loved having fairy lights in her hospital room whenever she was hospitalized. She had them in her room in North Carolina. While there, Jen looked forward to seeing fireflies. Since she was hospitalized in April, she never got to see them. I tried videoing them for her, but they appeared at dusk, so my phone wouldn't capture their light very well. One can only imagine the joy she got from those little lights. I wonder, do they have fireflies in heaven?

· Four ·

My Jennifer

Jeanette McKenna

I cannot tell you when I met Jennifer. It was probably 19 years ago. Our Son brought her to the house. It was a long ride from her home in Bakersfield, California, to our home. The land of oil wells and cows! This is how I describe Bakersfield.

Our Son told me she worked in a gun store, selling guns and ammo. Really? Found out her Dad was in law enforcement, and she grew up around guns. Her Dad took her shooting and fishing. So, she knew her stuff. We had a home in the country, up in Northern California. We built it from scratch. Clearing the land and burning brush were our weekend jobs. When Jennifer arrived, it was nearly done and looked awesome.

The Honda Element pulled in the driveway that weekend day. Out she jumped, with Pudge, our Son's dog. Pudge loved her right away. She always smelled good. The two of them greeted me with hugs and licks. Our Son commented, "Here she is!". Unpacking the Element came bags of stuff, food, dog bowls, dog bed, and so on. I soon discovered Jennifer had baggage. I did not realize how much stuff she had with her health condition, called cystic fibrosis (CF for short).

In between smiles and jokes, she coughed. And I mean coughed! I never knew someone other than myself who could cough more than I did! I discovered she also had asthma. With my cough and asthma, the love of chocolates, the love of Coke, we got along great!

Jennifer loved food. She ate more than all of us put together. Our Son commented when they went out to dinner; she ate more than he. Jennifer, Jen for short, was beautiful. Her black hair, creamy complexion, beautiful smile, one would never know she was as sick as this disease claimed. Her positive attitude through all her health challenges was an inspiration.

Two years went by, and soon wedding plans were in the works. Her engagement ring was sparkling gorgeous! They planned to marry on New Year's Day. So, no one would forget this day, and they would receive cards and well wishes. They were so "in love." A marriage made in heaven. Indeed, God had His hand in this marriage. It made my heart happy!

Jen visited her CF doctor in Pasadena, California. Quite a drive from Bakersfield. Some days they had to spend the night in the area due to appointments. Then the next day, on the way home, they would stop at Magic Mountain Amusement Park. Her doctor visits were exhausting, but Jen kept up with her husband and never complained. Pudge, their dog, waited by the front door till they reached home. Pudge loved Jen. She always smelled good.

They were married in 2005 in beautiful Cambria on the Coast of California. This indeed was a day the Lord had made. And so, life continued. Jen continued her college education and working at the gun shop. Our Son continued his education at Santa Barbara University and obtained his Ph.D. in Education. The happy couple traveled on many trips. Jen's health remained silent. In May 2006, we traveled with Jen's family on a cruise to the Hawaiian Islands. It was indeed a trip of a lifetime. I took numerous pictures and collected them in a forever album. As a family, we shared many fun visits.

Living in Bakersfield played havoc on Jen's CF. But Jen continued her strength and trust in the Lord. Our Son and Jen decided to find employment up North and decided to live in Idaho. He worked at the University, and Jen continued at the gun shop online. Later she worked at the Union Gospel Mission. Jen had a close relationship with the Lord. He guided her all her life with health issues. Her strength in Him continued to help other unfortunate individuals at the Mission. She also volunteered at Church and became a faithful, loyal member.

Around the year 2015, our Son suggested we relocate to Idaho. We purchased a home near their home. When Dad traveled back and forth from CA, Jen never forgot to stop and visit him. They drove around to different areas. Even to gun shops. When the dinner hour rolled around, they stopped at Panda Express for a take-out meal. Dad loved Jen.

As years passed, our Son became involved in sports activities, involving triathlons, marathons, bike races, etc. Jen followed along and was always at the sidelines cheering her husband with her duck call. Many times, she would ride her bike near the finish line. We shared some of these events with them in AZ, Utah, CA, and even Hawaii for the Kona Ironman!

All of a sudden, Jen's life took a turn for the worse. They were on a trip to Alaska, and Jen became ill. She was flown to the hospital in Washington from Alaska. She had contracted a bacterial infection that stopped her short! The doctors sent her home with oxygen and instructions to remain on the couch with oxygen, and there she stayed. As Jen goes through this, she leaned on God. Her heart and faith stayed fixed on Him. Still, with a smile, she never complained.

At this point, she might have known God was calling. Jen never did recover. She was 41 years old and on oxygen 24 hours per day. She did not travel much, except to our house for dinner. Our Son worked out of town three days a week, so her girlfriends stayed with her throughout those three days.

When Jen's CF Doctors suggested she apply for a pair of new lungs, she accepted. Jen wanted those new lungs!! "Just imagine breathing on my own," she'd say. This must have been exciting.

February 2019 came along, and our Son and Jen packed up and flew to Chapel Hill, North Carolina to the UNC Medical Center. They had rented a small house along with Jen's Mother and with a car. They could travel back and forth to the Medical Center. Jen would begin physical therapy to build up her endurance. With the help from the Lord, she did well. Thus, continuing her incredible journey for a pair of new lungs.

Hundreds of get-well cards of encouragement filled the mailbox; Friends prayed for her strength continuously. Jen sent videos to all of us back home. Her story touched many hearts. People she never met sent cards and prayers.

Weeks grew into months; Jen had been placed on a waitlist. May finally arrived, and so did a pair of new lungs. It was just her size. Tests were done, and she went into surgery. Surgery was performed in the middle of the night for twelve long hours. Our Son caught a late flight and arrived at the hospital as Jen was moved to recovery. She opened her eyes and smiled. Then, breathing on her own with her new lungs. This was a gift from God. No doubt about it!

A few weeks passed, Jen then suffered complications from years of CF, which took a toll on her other organs. A shock to all of us, not expecting difficulties. The doctors tried everything they could. Nurses checked on Jen's vitals every five minutes. Jen did not recover. She passed away peacefully with her husband and family by her side. At that moment, her transition into eternal life was truly special. She was totally at peace.

Jen had a joyful spirit. God's presence always surrounded her. We all were blessed to have her in our life for forty-one years. Especially her parents. Jen's passing will have an everlasting effect on all of our lives.

Our home is filled with pictures of Jen. I carry a memory of her with me every day. I know this will give me peace. I know the true love she and our Son had for each other and will remain close to his heart. Jen was genuinely gifted – a ray of sunshine. Some people journey through life and leave footprints of kindness, love, courage, compassion, joy, and faith. Even then, they continue to inspire us. May God bless us in our loving memory.

· Five ·

At A Crossroads

Galen Norsworthy

The classroom door opened. In walked two young ladies whom I had never met before. One was particularly striking with her bright eyes and a smile that lit up the room. The class was about to start, so I decided to wait until it was over to meet them. It was not unusual for strangers to come to the class.

Word had spread around Bakersfield that our college/career group, known as "Crossroads," offered more than just activities and a devotional tack-on. This was by design. When my wife, Lita, and I were being interviewed for leading this ministry, we told them that we wanted to bring seminary-level training to the college group with activities as a tack-on. And so, we did. Soon the half a dozen students in attendance grew to almost 75 each week. By their consistent attendance, they demonstrated that they were serious students of the Word of God.

While teaching the class that night, I would occasionally glance in the two visitors' directions to see if they were tracking. Not only were they taking copious notes, but the girl's eyes with the big smile seemed to sparkle with delight.

I knew then that they would not be just one-time visitors but were genuinely interested in becoming a part of the ministry.

This was confirmed when the class ended.

Both girls came excitedly up to me to introduce themselves. With a big smile, the girl said, "Hi, I'm Jennifer Ellis, and this is my friend, Sheerah White." This began a long and lasting relationship with the Bible at the center of it.

It was sometime later that I learned of Jennifer's medical condition. She had been suffering from cystic fibrosis since birth. While debilitating at times, especially when fighting a cold or the flu, she never lost her enthusiasm to learn and interact with whatever biblical lessons we were studying at the time – from soteriology to ecclesiology, to eschatology, to hamartiology, and the other disciplines of systematic theology.

Months went by, and then I noticed Jennifer started to miss a few Bible studies and activities. She came to me to explain that she was taking some college classes to get her teaching certificate. Since the classes were being recorded, she asked for copies so that she wouldn't miss anything. This pleased me as well and deepened our bond of friendship and mutual respect.

One night, Jen came to class all bubbly and wanted to introduce me to a young man. I was always skeptical and cautious when one of the students got into a romantic relationship with someone I didn't know. Too often, we would see this attraction become a distraction to their spiritual walk, and they would drop out of Bible study only to return later full of regret.

My wife and I expressed our concerns to her, but she assured us that would not be the case. He was her instructor at school and was also interested in coming to class with her when he could. That sounded good to me.

True to her word, she brought this young man one night to class and introduced him. "This is Corey. He's my friend, and also he's my professor," she said. It didn't take Corey long to prove to me that he was interested in Jennifer and in studying the Bible. Based on this, I relaxed and watched their relationship develop.

One day, in 2004, Corey and Jennifer came to Lita and me to make an announcement. He had asked her to become his wife. He was well aware of the difficulties their marriage would face with her health issues, but that wasn't going to be a problem, he said. They would do it together. Not wanting to assume anything, I asked them who they wanted to officiate at their wedding. They gave each other a knowing glance, and with a smile, Corey pointed to me. I felt humbled and privileged.

The evangelical pastors in Bakersfield had committed that they would conduct a minimum of twelve pre-marital sessions before conducting the wedding. I explained this to Corey and Jennifer, knowing it would take some focused effort given everyone's busy schedule.

"Not a problem," said Corey. "We'll make it work."

And it did.

On a cold January 1st, 2005 morning in Cambria, Corey and Jennifer exchanged their wedding vows on the coast of central California. It was my delight to announce them to the shivering audience as "husband and wife."

Jennifer loved being around guns. Whenever I would stop by the Second Amendment Sports in Bakersfield, I looked for her. She would always greet me with that big smile of hers and eyes wide with excitement and anticipation.

One day I noticed that she seemed a little down. So, I asked her if she was feeling okay. She replied, "Yeah," but her answer lacked her usual enthusiasm. Later she asked if we could talk. It was then that she shared what was on her heart. She had uncovered a crime being committed at work. What grieved her was that the person involved professed to be a Christian and even went to the church where I ministered. Jen knew she had to report it and would possibly have to testify in court, but what bothered her was the potential fallout this might have with a person's marriage and with a church where she was a volunteer.

I counseled her to "Just do what you know is right and leave the rest to the Lord." But that was just like Jen, always concerned about others and what her actions might have on their lives.

A few years later, Corey and Jennifer informed us that they had decided to relocate to Coeur d'Alene, Idaho. Corey had competed in an Ironman competition there and noticed how clear and clean the air was. It might help Jen with her breathing. He was able to land a professorship at a nearby college, so the move was finalized.

Lita and I were able to visit with them while on a road trip from Seattle. After having a delightful breakfast on the waterfront with them, Jennifer asked if we would like to see where she did volunteer work, and of course, we said "Yes."

We followed her as we drove around the city and eventually pulled into a parking lot in an area that at first seemed a little sketchy. If I remember correctly, it was a Union Gospel Mission that provided services for women and children. While the name seems to escape me, Jennifer's reception as she walked in the front door is still vivid in my mind. It was like her presence lit up the room. Everyone who saw her immediately smiled. That was the impact she had on them. She proudly introduced us to the staff as her college pastor and wife from Bakersfield and concluded with "He's the one who married us!" and ended the introduction with her contagious smile.

Time spent with Corey and Jen always seemed rushed and short as we tried to catch each other up on the events of our lives. One day, we received an invitation from Corey to come to Coeur d'Alene for a surprise birthday party for Jen. We weren't sure if our schedule would allow it, but the opportunity opened up when I worked and was on the Board of Directors decided to hold their annual meeting in Bend, Oregon. We decided we could make a partial business trip out of this and affirmed to Corey that we would try to be there.

Not much caught Jen by surprise, even a "birthday party" that wasn't on her actual birthday. However, I still recall how she reacted when Lita and I parked down the street from their house with a smile on my face. She was supposed to be in the backyard with her other guests but just happened to come out to the front as we were getting out of my truck. From down the street, I heard her call my name "GALEN!!!" She attempted to run to us but started having difficulty breathing. We told her to wait that we would come to her. Then came the smiles and hugs.

It was a fun and enjoyable party as we reconnected with her relatives, many of whom we had not seen since the wedding. Little did we know that the next time we would all be together again in Coeur d'Alene to celebrate Jen's life as she was finally breathing unhindered in heaven.

Special Note: Galen Norsworthy passed away on May 9, 2020. He was a giant among men in faith, hope, and love. He was a Disciple in Christ, a husband, a dad, a soldier, a teacher, and a mentor. He lived every calling in his life with purpose and conviction. It was an honor and privilege to call you a friend and brother in Christ. You are up in heaven with Jen, laughing it up I am sure talking about whatever. We will meet again soon!

• Six •

God's Symphony in My Life

Jackie Maker

Jen McKenna was my cherished friend. I met Jen in 2012 by volunteering and working at Union Gospel Mission Center for Women and Children in Coeur d'Alene. We had instant friendship chemistry. You know the kind where you almost instantly feel like you've been friends since you were kids. We had it. Jen's dry sense of humor, sense of adventure, and love for people drew me to her. I profoundly felt we were kindred spirits, and Jen told me that she felt the same on many occasions.

As Jen and I trusted each other more and more, we shared deeper and deeper parts of ourselves, our pain, and our stories. Over time our wonderful husbands met, and we shared a beautiful friendship full of food, fun, and travel. Jen and Corey became cherished confidants and partners in crime to my husband Mike and me.

Early on in our friendship Jen shared with me that she had suffered from depression and wanted to be healed from it; we began praying for each other and praying specifically for this area. Over the next three years, I watched Jen and supported her as she very purposely began working on areas of her life that she knew were contributing to depression. With our tight group of girlfriends, Jan Vetter, Amanda Morgan, and Robin Olson, Jen was on a mission to grow closer to Christ and grow in her confidence in the woman she was, and the unique gift's she had been created to use. I celebrated with her, as did our tight group of girlfriends as she walked out of depression and was emotionally healed. Jen immediately began looking for ways to share with others who struggled with emotional pain. She began leading Genesis recovery groups, met one on one with women in need of a word of encouragement, prayer, and truth. Jen built many new friendships with people of all ages and was always on the lookout for someone to encourage and to love. I was amazed watching her collect people wherever she went: people of all sizes, shapes, financial status, belief system, friendly, grouchy, and everything in between. She lived as a missionary to the people in her life. Sharing with each of us the peace she had from God, insecurities when she felt them, and hope for our own lives, especially in the areas we couldn't imagine God changing.

Over the past year, Jen and I even began a mentoring relationship with two younger women in our church who had two children under 4. In the beginning, we often wondered if, as childless women, we would have anything to offer them. Our friendship with these women grew quickly, and we soon discovered the many things we shared as women, daughters, wives, and friends. Jen continued pursuing these relationships online and through texting after she left for her lung transplant in North Carolina. Jen was focused and driven to build meaningful, healthy, and God-centered relationships everywhere she went.

When I tell others about Jen, I have always said Jen never lived as a 'Sick Person.' Jen lived, loved, and laughed her life to the fullest. Jen loved deeply, authentically, and with her whole heart. Jen made me feel like I hung the moon in her eyes. She spoke blessing, love, and truth into my life regularly. We rarely disagreed about anything, and she periodically told me the truth if I was beefing stubborn, selfish, or short-sighted in a given situation. We had running jokes that sounded like complete nonsense to others. Jen told the truth in our relationship even when it was hard, and I witnessed her doing this with other relationships as well.

Jen made me laugh so hard at times that my sides hurt. There was a time Mike and I, Jen and Corey went on a double date. Due to CF, Jen sometimes passed gas loudly at unlikely times. On this occasion, a young, charming male waiter took our dinner order, and he got to Jen. As Jen opened her mouth to speak, she passed gas very loudly. The look on the poor waiter's face was hilarious and something I will never forget! Jen, with total grace, said,' *Well, that was awkward'* and proceeded to give her order. Jen was known for her great sense of humor and her big beautiful smile, and knee-slapping laughter. We loved it.

Jen had an incredible way of making you feel like you were loved, known, and accepted by her. Jen had this kind of friendship with my husband (her other big brother), and they had many funny and off-color inside jokes, deeply thoughtful conversations, and hours of tv & movie trivia one-liners between them.

Jen's perseverance and commitment to relationships and get the most out of every situation even when adversity arose was something I learned most from her. On another double date night, we were out to dinner, and she and I got up to go to the ladies' room. Jen began to cough on the way to the bathroom and couldn't get her breath; she began to pass out. I held Jen up, and a waiter went to get an office chair on rollers they had. When Jen gained her breath out, she had tears in her eyes. She said, '*I am having dinner here tonight! That was scary, but I am not missing our night out!* I then rolled Jen in the office chair through the busy restaurant back to our table, and we had our dinner and dessert. When the bill came, the waiter told us someone had paid Corey and Jen's tab. They were stunned. The waiter said the 'payer' had heard Jen and saw her struggle and wanted her to know they were cheering her on. Jen had that effect on people. People couldn't help but cheer her on because she shined hope and perseverance everywhere she went.

I had the honor of being with Jen in North Carolina the week before she passed away. Jen's gift of impacting everyone around her with her witty humor, huge smile, and love for people was present in every inch of her hospital room. In the most challenging moments of her life physically, Jen continued to love others well. Her last text to me was about praying for me and encouraging me. Jen has left an incredible investment in my life. Her love for Jesus, desire to honor him and glorify and magnify His name in everything she did inspire me never to give up. To not sweat the small stuff and continue to love others around me even when it's hard.

A few months before she left for North Carolina to await her surgery, Jen shared about her upcoming journey towards transplant -Jen said that God had shown her that He had been warming people up for their roles in this journey for a long time. Jen said that God had shown her that he had given each of us a piece of music to learn, even her and Corey. She said that God was the conductor and would pull all of the music together into his masterpiece. Jen said that when all was said and done, people would look at her story and all God did and recognize it as His work as his masterpiece. Jen is God's masterpiece, and I will always feel honored, blessed, and glad He allowed me to have her in my life.

Every word that God spoke to Jen was life to her. She didn't want to miss one word. Jen was my bestie, and I was hers. She was God's symphony in my life. Her music is still playing today.

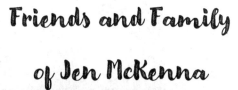

Friends and Family of Jen McKenna

· Seven ·

A Quiet Joy

Jessica Morgan

The song, *I'll Rejoice*, was inspired by a family friend. Her name was Jen, and she was the brightest person in every sense, but she suffered her whole life from cystic fibrosis. My husband's sister, Amanda, introduced us several years ago at the Ironman triathlon in Coeur d'Alene. She was cheering on her husband, sitting on the sidewalk downtown with her portable oxygen, waiting for him to come by. Her sincerity and easy laughter immediately warmed us. You could be your utterly weird self around her, and she would join right in. And despite her daily fight against the disease, she embraced life, ran half marathons, cycled, hiked, and volunteered.

Last year, Jen passed away after a lung transplant. On our drive home from her memorial service, my husband and I ruminated on a favorite verse someone had shared of hers: *"This is the day the Lord has made. Let us rejoice and be glad in it." – Psalm 118:24*

They said she would use this verse to get through the hard days, that it was a sort of "life verse." As she consistently faced suffering, we were in awe that she chose to rejoice in the day – not because of how she felt, but because God made it. That evening I wrote the first few lines of "I'll Rejoice."

As more of the song unfolded, my husband and I found ourselves remembering others who had passed in recent years: his father, a dear coworker, a friend's mother, all of our grandparents. And for many of those goodbyes, I was singing – in hospital rooms, at memorial services, leading church congregations, in our home. Song is what I can bring into the dark spaces. However, it's not really about the song, how it suspends us for a moment so we can feel...or not feel.

But during those hard times of loss, I have felt something unexpected. A quiet *joy*, of all things, seems to linger with the grief. It fills the sorrowful gaps with meaning. When we lose people, the pain honors the beautiful weight of their existence. The quiet joy exists *because their life meant something*.

I suppose I've learned from Jen and writing this song that rejoicing – gladness – is still possible as we suffer. It can exist, not because we have a good reason or a feeling to inspire us, but because we're alive and it matters, and God gives us another day.

Lyrics from *I'll Rejoice*.

Written by Jessica and Shane Morgan.

Performed by The Good Fridays, a collaborative music project Jessica helped start.

This is the day the Lord has made
I'll rejoice, I'll rejoice

This is the day the Lord has made
I'll rejoice — in everything
Do you see the clouds?
Feel the rain from Heaven.
He is with you now.
Can you hear the breaking morning?
It's rejoicing...

This is the day the Lord has made
I'll rejoice, I'll rejoice
This is the day the Lord has made
I'll rejoice — in everything
Think of those you love.
Their caring arms surround you.
And through all the world
You can hear the joy and laughter
people singing...

This is the day the Lord has made
I'll rejoice, I'll rejoice
This is the day the Lord has made
I'll rejoice — in everything
He who made us made this world.
Brother, sister we behold .

This is the day. This is divine.
This is the day the Lord has made
I'll rejoice — in everything

· Eight ·

Lean In

Lauren Penston

I first met Jen at the Welcome Center at our church. I had seen her around my brother's work at UGM, where we ran into each other, and I recognized her from around the church. But what caught my eye this time was the gigantic knife peeking out of her front jean pocket. Well, I guess it wasn't as much looking as it was screaming, "Hey! I've a knife!" and being an avid knife carrier, I just had to ask. Jen was stoked to whip that bad boy out and show me all the unique things about it. She told me about why she chose it, traded it with a co-worker in Bakersfield, and how long she wanted it. In what must have been just a couple of minutes, I learned a lot; I remember she was wearing Doc Martens, skinny jeans, and a *Firefly* t-shirt. Now I'm a people watcher, always have been; maybe it's just the introvert in me trying to figure out how to connect, or perhaps it's the slight bit of sociopathic tendencies to figure out how things work by taking them apart bit by bit, people included. Still, in those short minutes, I got to SEE Jen. Yes, it was casual and fun, but she was vulnerable, and that was something I had long tried to figure out how to be, so I was curious. Then, of course, I realized she had asked me a question and had no idea what it was. I awkwardly asked her what she said. She wanted to know if I carried a knife, I do, and what I liked about it, didn't like, and so on. We went on to complain about women's pants and how the pockets never fit the important stuff, *cough* knives, hence why I had even seen the knife in the first place! We ended up making a plan to meet up for coffee and talk more about knives. It was short, easy, casual, but genuine and intimate. I instantly felt a connection.

We met later that week and chatted for several hours; we both had lived in the Bakersfield area, so we had something in common. From there, I learned more about her over the next few months as she joined our youth staff as a leader, and we got to hang out more. I learned about her history, the jobs she had worked, and how she and her husband Corey had met and fell in love. We talked about different old movies we liked and what TV shows we were addicted to. *Criminal Minds* was one of our favorites. Every once in a while, in conversation, she would start coughing hard, and it was a little while later I learned about CF. I would always get nervous and concerned whenever she went into a coughing fit, so I asked her to come up with a code word to know when she needed help. The first word she said was a hotdog. I cracked up because who thinks of that?! But that's Jen.

As the years passed, I got to know Jen really well; she was always a person I could talk to. Sometimes we would text each other movie quotes to see if we could guess. Other times we would notice one of our favorite actors showing up as a cameo in another series. In recent years we talked a lot about depression and the *Genesis Process* that she had gone through to find healing. As we grew closer, I began to fit together how she was able to cultivate such a genuine relationship in what seemed like such an easy way. Intentionality. Jen took her commitments seriously, to people, to jobs, to her husband, to whatever she needed to. Above all, she took her relationship with Christ seriously. She was intentional with her time and her growth. For a while, she and another woman mentored a friend and me, so I got to see that growth firsthand. Jen made space for growth. She made space for change. She challenged the patterns that she had grown accustomed to in her life, both good and bad. She intentionally invited God into her choices, thought processes, behavior, and so on. She learned how to do that through The *Genesis Process.*

Jen taught me a lot. And I mean that with all sincerity. With Jen, I learned to laugh at myself, that it's okay to be silly and serious at the same time. We shared many moments that were filled with laughter and many serious moments. I could ask Jen about anything, and I took advantage of that. Through our years of friendship, I grew a lot. I was speaking of Jen recently, and I was reminded of how gentle she was with me. I have some coping defenses that have caused some stuck places in my life, and Jen saw through my defenses and led me out of them. But she was never forceful or abrupt. She loved me hard, and although I was resistant at first, she pushed forward. Through our interactions, I slowly learned to trust and started to figure out why these walls were so high in my life. She took time with me and was always intentional with our time together.

. Nine .

Just Breathe

Lana Jordan

When I found out Jen was getting a lung transplant, I was so excited for her, for us, for everyone who knew her! We made plans for me to fly up to visit and go kayaking. Jen couldn't wait for me to see how beautiful Idaho was. Our friendship all of these years meant the world to me. And it didn't matter if it had been five days or five years since we last spoke because she is always right there. I could hear her talk and see her smile. Her positive energy was always contagious.

A few years before, she was in Alaska with her husband for his Ironman competition. I know she loved to cheer him on. She got to ride in a helicopter to the hospital. This was serious, but coming from her, it was more of an adventure. She wasn't feeling well, another infection attacking her lungs. I spoke with her mom every six weeks when I groomed her dog, Squirt. She and her husband were talking about going up to install a special water system in her house. It would kill any bacteria in the water that could get in her lungs from just taking a shower.

Her mom is so strong. I know where she gets it from. It takes a lot even to get a hint of worry or that things were getting rough from talking to her. This talk seems to be one of those times. I tried to make a plan to come from my first visit up to Idaho. My husband wanted to make all my travel arrangements for my birthday and make sure that he was home for our kids while I was away. Jen wanted me to wait just a little bit so that she could feel better and enjoy my visit. Then it was starting to turn cold, and she talked me into staying until the weather was warmer so he wouldn't be cooked up inside; plus, by then, Jen would be better and be able to do a lot more. No doubts from me because I could hear her voice and see her smile.

Pretty soon, Spring came. It was time to plan that trip. Jen's health had fluctuated, and she was not where she wanted to be. She was trying to be active with the church and volunteer on good days. She was busy but not enough by her standards. A few things were coming up that she was positive she would be able to make it to, so we decided to wait until Fall. I thought maybe by then I could be there and help drive her around or help with anything she needed while your husband was working. Fall came and went. She had the volunteer work that she would do at the church anytime she could. It seemed if she wasn't in the hospital, she was out living life to the fullest. I'm sure she was a light to so many people.

By this time, I had groomed Squirt a few times without Virginia being there. She was up in Idaho helping her. I called to check on her, and she was so excited because she could vacuum a room. It had been a while, but I knew even doing just that, she would exhaust herself. I called another time, and she was excited because she walked across the whole room unassisted. None of this seemed right. She ran a marathon and always had energy. She was nonstop between church, volunteer work, going with her husband to Ironman competitions, trips, and training. Sure, she would cough some, but that never slowed down, not for this long. Then someone came to pick her up for church. She was so happy to talk to me and would do it again soon. I could see that smile just by hearing her voice.

Not long after that, she let me know that getting a lung transplant might be an option. She was so excited. Trips were made to meet with a few hospitals and coordinators. Then COTA was going to help with organizing the costs, paying bills, and getting donations. I wanted to help somehow. I wanted to spread the word and help get as many donations as possible so she could focus on herself instead of the costs involved with living in a different place while getting ready for the transplant.

Just Breathe. Most people knew the Faith Hill song, *Just Breathe*. This had a whole new meaning. Just to breathe without struggle is what we all wanted for her. I could already see her taking deep breaths with her new lungs and pushing everything to the limit just because she finally could. To just breathe and take in all God's glory around her.

To me, she was fearless and unstoppable.

I had a plan and talked it over with her. I met with a girl I knew that designed shirts and did fundraisers. I typed out a brief letter and order form and was on my way to get those donations that she needed. I started talking to people, and I received orders and donations from close friends and family. Then, I posted on social media about her and the fundraiser. Every day I handed out the letter to my clients, usually seeing 2 to 4 per day. I was so excited to tell them about Jen McKenna, my fearless friend since grade school. She was working so hard, pushing how many steps she could take, trying to keep her strength up. Jen had to work all day trying to get strong enough for the transplant. She had to be ready at any minute if she got the call for a transplant; all while praying for the family's that were losing someone they loved.

I was talking with one of my clients. She had a friend in high school that had CF. Her face lit up while she was talking about her friend. She was always so positive, a joy to be around, and always smiling, just like Jen. Then she let me know her friend had passed away right after her 18th birthday. A few other clients had similar stories. They all cherished their friends that had passed away too young.

It got me thinking back to junior high. I didn't even remember meeting Jen. We were just automatically friends. We were not the girly girls who were into impressing boys. We just wanted to be kids and have fun. It was so nice having a friend who would accidentally rip one and just shrug it off. I'm sure Jen told me the extra toots and bubbles were from her medication, but I didn't care. Sometimes she would cough, then cough some more; we would look at each other and start laughing as the burps and farts made way. We always had fun. She showed me her bow and arrow. She invited me to one of her archery competitions. Jen was such a badass, walking around with a bow that was only about a foot shorter than her. Being a bit intimidating to me, but she walked around like she knew everyone or would soon enough. She held her head high but never look down on anyone and always smiled.

As we got into high school, I think she tried to hide her bodily noises a little more. Somehow, she had a positive vibe all the time and confidence about her the others didn't have. She was so bright, always in different clubs to challenge her brain. She could walk up and talk to anybody. Never shy. She was so confident. She treated everyone like a friend. Several people weren't so nice, but she would just say to ignore them because they probably had something going on in their life that wasn't so pleasant.

When my parents found out about her fundraiser, they wanted to contribute. The first time my dad ran into her, working at the local gun shop, he was so excited. It would help if she was packing. She was always a badass. Sure, it was a lot easier than carrying a bow and arrow around. I know my dad would go to the gun shop extra just to say hi to her.

Along with exchanging a few jokes, she always had a comeback or a witty remark that would have my dad laughing. The next time I would see my dad, he would have a smile ear to ear telling me that he saw her. She was always his favorite. I ran into the gun shop when she wasn't there one time. There was an older fellow at the counter asking one of the younger guys where she was. They offered to help him but couldn't. He needed an expert like Jen. Someone that took pride in their work and learned as much as they could.

She spent another week talking with more of my clients. It would bring up memories that I had forgotten, like when she came over before she moved. My boys were about 7 and 9. They wanted to go to watch a superhero movie. I decided we could dress up in Halloween costumes just for the fun of it. I asked if she wanted a costume, and she was all in! She did not question why on Earth we would dress up, especially since it wasn't Premiere Week. That was the pinkest I had ever seen her in, especially with no camo in it. She pulled off the pink fairy, even though a Lara Croft or Hawkeye would have been more suitable. We even went for lunch after. All in costume! Such a fun day, and we were all smiles.

The fundraiser was going great. Jen received the call in late May to get ready for her transplant. It was happening this time.! She was going to breathe!

I booked my flight to visit. Then everything changed. There were complications. Nothing seemed real. Jen never gave up. Looking back, I saw the struggles she must have gone through. The insecurities she must have had, but she didn't let them show. She was always true to herself. She loved, always trying, always learning, always giving her love and knowledge to help others. I can only imagine the Angel she has become. Real wings, and I'm sure they're not pink. She was a true warrior and a true friend. I love her and miss her. Now she can just breathe. I can't hear her voice, but I know she is always smiling.

· Ten ·

The Front Row

Kurt Staeuble

The first time I met Jen McKenna was when she showed up at church on a Sunday morning for a class, I was leading on the topic of Peace-Making and Conflict Resolution. In that initial meeting, three things about Jen stood out that morning. First, she sat in the front row, which is fairly uncommon for most of the classes I teach. For some reason, people seem to have an aversion to sitting up close to the teacher. Second, Jen's hair was still a bit wet, as if she'd rushed to church. Third, she had a bit of a cough, which I chalked up to a cold.

I remember thinking, "So, who is this person who just showed up to class?" Also, I wondered if she would return the following week. Which she did! And Jen still sat in the front row, still had wet hair, and still had a cough. In fact, during the second class, Jen had a pretty intense coughing fit. At this point, my hunch was her coughs weren't simply the result of a common cold.

As the 8-week class went on, Jen became more engaged in the conversation. She offered several insights into the class discussion. She also revealed a strong sense of humor, one that I would describe with words such as *random*, *satirical*, and *sideways*. Jen loved to look at life from a unique perspective.

As time went on, Jen became more involved in the life of our church. By this time, I learned that CF was the cause of Jen's constant battle to attain oxygen. It was tough watching a woman in her thirties have such a difficult time breathing. But I also learned that Jen wasn't looking for pity. She wanted to be involved in life, rather than relegated to the sidelines. So, Jen made every effort to take part in whatever was going on.

From my perspective, the biggest shift in Jen's life (both emotionally and spiritually) occurred when she began volunteering at the Union Gospel Mission. I think I can honestly say that Jen was getting as much out of her service to the women and children at UGM as she was giving to them. UGM is a place for rescue, recovery, and restoration. And, as is often the case with UGM volunteers, we sometimes learn we require spiritual growth and healing as much as the program residents. Jen sought to absorb as much learning as she could, and it was obvious to those around her that her life was taking on a new, healthy trajectory. Jen's development was so marked, UGM brought her on staff to serve as a volunteer coordinator.

Jen also joined our church staff in a small, part-time role as a media assistant. Jen made sure our visuals for Sunday morning were always ready to go. She also got involved in helping us organize our computer hardware and systems. One thing I learned about Jen: she had a real knack for cannibalizing an old computer!

Jen was a blast to have at staff meetings. She always made things real and down-to-earth. She brought a perfect balance of serious input and goofball humor to our gatherings. She was at her best whenever we celebrated a staff birthday. Jen would come up with all sorts of crazy ideas to make the party more fun and goofier. Because Jen and I shared an appreciation for the TV show *Better Call Saul*, she themed my birthday around elements of the show. Just as Saul led a Bingo game for senior citizens, Jen brought in a Bingo game for us to play.

In the summer of 2017, Sara and I traveled with Jen and Corey to Alaska to serve as a support crew for Corey as he competed in the Alaskaman triathlon. At first, everything went great as we arrived in Anchorage and then traveled south to Seward. I remember we stopped at REI to get snacks and such and had a fun time roaming the store. In Seward, we settled into our 2-bedroom condo and then went out for dinner at the harbor.

But the next day we went out to lunch and Jen asked Corey to pull the car to the front of the restaurant rather than walk to the car. I couldn't help but note the car was parked some 50 yards from the restaurant entrance. That was a clue that she was having a bad breathing day. But Jen didn't complain at all.

Later that evening, Sara and I went out for a walk to the harbor. As we were on our way back, we got a call from Corey that he had taken Jen to the ER in Seward. The expectation was

Jen would get some sort of treatment and be back at the condo in no time flat. But that's not the way things went. Instead, Jen was airlifted to Anchorage and admitted to the hospital. The Alaskaman plans went out the window and all the attention was now squarely on Jen. Jen did stabilize at the hospital, but she and Corey would have to stay a few days beyond our scheduled departure time. So, without Jen and Corey, Sara and I headed back to Idaho.

After returning from Alaska, Jen would have a few more hospital stays due to severe reactions to the CF infections. And every time I would go to see her, Jen would always put her best face forward. Even in times of physical and emotional challenge, Jen thought about serving the person who had come to visit her.

Our church staff meetings typically take place on Wednesdays. One time I remember getting a phone call from Jen on a Wednesday morning. I knew she had been feeling really bad and expected her to inform me she couldn't make the meeting. Which I understood. Instead, Jen was calling from the church parking lot. She asked me to bring a wheelchair to get her so she could get to the meeting. As physically hard as it was for her to be at our meeting, it was harder for her not to be engaged with people.

As was the case for everyone who loved Jen, news of her passing hit us hard. Our adult son (Aaron) with Downs syndrome was especially saddened. I remember heading into his room the morning we learned of Jen's passing and sharing the difficult news with him. Aaron immediately bowed his head and wept. Jen and Aaron worked together at UGM, and over time they had built a special relationship. I had the honor of leading Jen's memorial service. It was a beautiful time of sharing and memories. Here are the words I shared for the message:

Although I have had a lot of time to put this message together, I put it off until early this week. I believe the reason for this sort of pastoral procrastination was that I subconsciously felt like writing out my thoughts would mean that Jen was really gone. And I just didn't feel like admitting it was really true. Jen was truly one of those individuals of whom we say, "THEY LEFT US WAY TOO SOON."

My first memory of Jen was when she showed up for a Sunday morning class, I was teaching about dealing with conflict resolution. I'd never seen her before but was impressed she sat in the front row. Nobody sits in the front row! But Jen did, and for that reason she scored some early points with me.

Of course, in that first class, it was inevitable for Jen to have a coughing fit. I just figured she had a bad cold and try to roll with it. But the following week the same thing happened...but I still tried to play it cool. But, when Jen was once again gripped by a wicked coughing spell in the third class, I knew something was up.

Still, she didn't talk about it and I didn't ask. I just learned to take a pause in my teaching in order to give Jen a chance to recover. In time, I learned about her struggle with CF, although it seemed she could have some stretches where she experienced a little relief. Jen was a great student to have in class because she got involved and asked really good questions.

I always appreciate someone who engages in one of my classes! As time went on, I got to know Jen, along with Corey, better.

Now, from the get-go I knew Jen was different. My word for her would be quirky. She had interests that were a bit more unusual for women. Guns and knives come to mind. When I learned about her affinity for knives, I told Jen she had to meet my daughter, Lauren, who shared a similar passion for anything with a sharp blade.

As time passed, it came about that Jen joined our church staff to help us in the areas of computer/media/tech/graphics. Let me say it was amazing to see the way she could cannibalize old computers to make repairs!

In a selfish way, I miss Jen because I can have a very sideways sense of humor, and Jen would get my quips and jokes that sailed over the heads of most. It was nice to know there was someone else who was a bit twisted in the brain!

I definitely have to tip my hat to Jen's tenacity. There would be times she would show up for a staff meeting when most would have called it a day. More than once, Jen would call me as she was on her way to church and ask if I could meet her in the parking lot with a wheelchair so I could roll her to the elevator. I think most would agree that one of the most painful things about being Jen's friend was that for a woman of such wit, compassion, creativity and vitality, her body wasn't in the mood to cooperate. As Jen was growing as a human being, her body was going in a different direction. Jen certainly did all she could to try and kick her body into gear. But sometimes the infections were just too much to handle.

Gathered here today is a multitude of people who have stories of how Jen impacted their life in one way or another...despite her physical condition! A section of scripture that comes to my mind when thinking about Jen's ability to touch lives in spite of her illness comes from 2 Corinthians 4.

The context of the passage is simple. The Apostle Paul is sharing how missionary life is hard. Really hard! It seems wherever he goes some people respond well to the message of the Gospel, but others...not so much.

So much so, that he describes his difficulties with incredible clarity:

2 Corinthians 4

[7] But we have this treasure in jars of clay, to show that the surpassing power belongs to God and not to us. [8] We are afflicted in every way, but not crushed; perplexed, but not driven to despair; [9] persecuted, but not forsaken; struck down, but not destroyed; [10] always carrying in the body the death of Jesus, so that the life of Jesus may also be manifested in our bodies. [11] For we who live are always being given over to death for Jesus' sake, so that the life of Jesus also may be manifested in our mortal flesh. [12] So death is at work in us, but life in you.

Does that not sound like Jen?

A broken-down body, yet God working through her to encourage, bless and challenge those around her?

[13] Since we have the same spirit of faith according to what has been written, "I believed, and so I spoke," we also believe, and so we also speak, [14] knowing that he who raised the Lord Jesus will raise us also with Jesus and bring us with you into his presence. [15] For it is all for your sake, so that as grace extends to more and more people it may increase thanksgiving, to the glory of God.

Here Paul is saying that when the earthly body gives out, he had hope that one day he would leave his body behind and experience life in Heaven in the presence of God.

And check out these final thoughts of Paul on the matter:

[16] So we do not lose heart. Though our outer self is wasting away, our inner self is being renewed day by day. [17] For this light momentary affliction is preparing for us an eternal weight of glory beyond all comparison, [18] as we look not to the things that are seen but to the things that are unseen. For the things that are seen are transient, but the things that are unseen are eternal.

Allow me to read verse 16 one more time, because this is the verse that has, in my mind, Jen written all over it!!!

[16] So we do not lose heart. Though our outer self is wasting away, our inner self is being renewed day by day.

For the 5 plus years I knew Jen, that's what I got to witness.

The outer person of Jen was definitely wasting away. But the inner person of Jen was growing in all sorts of ways! Jen was a *person who grew so much, she became a person who was able to serve and minister to others. She did so in our church. She did so at UGM. And she also impacted lives in our community!*

May I just say, that's what the Gospel, the good news message of Jesus Christ looks like. It's the power to impact lives as a result of the inner change God does within us. Of what it means to be a true follower of Jesus, the apostle Paul wrote these words:

Therefore, if anyone is in Christ, he (or she) is a new creation. The old has passed away; behold, the new has come. (2 Corinthians 5:17)

In the short time I knew Jen, she positioned herself - submitted herself I might say - to truly be grown by God. Jen didn't just simply believe in the Gospel...she actually applied the Gospel promises of Jesus to her life. And you and I are the beneficiaries of her decision to "deep down" put her trust in God's ability to bring forth transformation in her life. I believe the reason this happened was because Jen, at a certain point in her life journey, got desperate enough for change. Jen found herself at a spiritual crossroads, and determined that maybe, just maybe, her creator knew better how to inform her life than she did.

May I say, as a pastor, I wish more people who claim the name of Jesus as Savior had the same sort of desperation that Jen displayed. Because Jen's desperation resulted in radical transformation. So, here on earth, Jen allowed God to have way with her inner person. I think most of us would agree that decision made Jen a better person! And now, Jen is experiencing another transformational promise of God. The promise that those who put their trust in Jesus won't have to worry about a body that struggles, and after so many years finally breaks down.

Isaiah 40:31 says this: But they who wait for the Lord shall renew their strength; they shall mount up with wings like eagles; they shall run and not be weary; they shall walk and not faint.

Today that is Jen's reality! But the reason Jen is experiencing such freedom is because she put her trust in Jesus and waited upon the Lord. On earth, Jen struggled to take in oxygen. But in the presence of her Lord, Jen is no longer laboring to breathe. And she's breathing in the wonder and glory and power and grace of her maker.

· Eleven ·

The Girl with the Thousand-Watt Smile

Mike McKenna

I first met Jen when our son, Corey, brought her to our house to meet her future in-laws. We lived in Northern California, in a small town called Shingletown. I am not sure what I expected when they arrived. But, out of the car stepped a short and thin girl with a thousand-watt smile, and I learned a personality to match over time.

On the weekend, we did a tour around the Shasta County area. We showed Jen the sights where Corey grew up. We went fishing in Eastern Shasta County. We learned a lot about her that weekend, as she did with us. We also learned how much Jen loved God, Corey, Pudge, monkeys, guns, fishing, Hello Kitty, and eating. Corey could not go wrong with a girl who loved the two best food groups: meat and cheese!

At first, it was hard to believe Jen was so sick until you heard her cough. Also, her daily routine of breathing treatments. She would put on a thing that looked like a flak vest. It vibrated her back and chest, which loosened mucus in her chest. She had more medications than any one person should ever have to take.

We traveled to Bakersfield to meet our future in-laws. In due course, a wedding was planned for January 1, 2005. It was a beautiful day, as was Jen. Corey and Jen were happy. Everyone had a good time at the wedding except the frogs who slipped off the wedding cake. Yes, frogs on a wedding cake, something you don't see at every wedding! Jen's idea, I'm sure.

During their time in Bakersfield, we made many trips to Bakersfield. Two things we always did was visit the Second Amendment Gun Store. This was Jen's store! We also visited Moo's Creamery. Perhaps, the world's best ice cream shop! Many times, I traveled to their house to dog sit Pudge.

For some reason, it always amused me to see Jen strap on that big 45-caliber pistol to her waist in preparation for work. Jen loved working at the gun store. I am sure they loved having her there too. After a few years, Corey and Jen decided to move to Coeur d'Alene, Idaho, for various reasons. One of which was better air for Jen. Now our trips were North instead of South. Jen did well in Coeur d'Alene for a while. She continued to work for the gun store online and a Bible Church she and Corey loved.

After visits to Coeur d'Alene, we decided to buy a home there. Corey found a home close to theirs. I started making trips there to work on this house. During these trips, Jen and I hung out. We took some road trips, had dinner together, and watched Big Bang Theory on television.

I don't think anyone meeting Jen for the first time knew how sick she really was. Jen had CF. It is not something you catch from anyone. It is something we are born with, until our death. CF is like the terminator. It cannot be reasoned with, or be killed, nor does it stop!

After our move to Coeur d'Alene, the decline in Jen's health was truly saddening. She was on oxygen 24/7 and could not walk more than fifteen feet without stopping to rest. She barely ate. When I saw she could not eat much, I knew she was in real trouble. She lost so much weight, a weight she could not afford. Jen's only hope was a double lung transplant. When her Doctors offered this option, she and Corey decided to go for it!

In February 2019, Jen was scheduled to go to North Carolina to begin the lung transplant process. She had a great send-off from her Church and the local community. Corey arranged the move, and Jen and her Mother relocated there. Corey made trips to be with her as much as he could.

In May, Jen got her new lungs and took her first breath ever with normal lungs. She was even able to sit up and walk. Then, her personal terminator returned with a vengeance Jen's thin, malnourished, frail body started to fail. Her surgery scars did not heal, her organs began to fail also. Jen did not recover. She passed away in the early morning hours on June 27, 2019, after a month-long battle with her personal terminator.

Imagine having an illness all your life, from the day you were born, that never really goes away but only gets worse. She fought her enemy with God's strength, the support of her husband and family, and good cheers and smiles. Jen lost the battle with CF, as everyone does. But she fought for forty-one years. This gal, the strongest, most courageous person I had ever known, was a thin, frail-looking gal with this thousand-watt smile!

• Twelve •

Daily Routines

Lindsey Pinckney

As years progress, a person with cystic fibrosis has to battle many obstacles. Each one is different. Each one presents its own challenge. Cystic fibrosis is a genetic mutation, one that contains more than 1,700 mutations – each presenting its own challenges. Both parents are carriers. There is no cure, but there is now medicine that can slow down the progression of it. Unfortunately, Jen was too old to take the new medicine, as her CF was too advanced. A person with CF has a daily routine of treatments and maintenance on top of just everyday living.

Early in life, Jen developed a bacterial infection that was difficult to eliminate. With the help of her amazing team at the CF clinic at Spokane's Sacred Heart Hospital and the Infectious Disease Hospital at the University of Washington, Jen was able to get a handle on some of the underlying issues with CF, including her bacterial infection. One amazing person who was part of this team, Lindsey Pinckney, researched new opportunities from a pharmacy standpoint. Lindsey's role at the clinic was CF Pharmacist Provider and she provides her perspective into the daily life of Jen's medicine journey.

From Lindsey Pinckney:

I am a list-maker. I list out my responsibilities and prioritize them down to the last detail. If you are anything like me, your list might look something like this on an average day (super packed and crazy):

- working
- housekeeping
- meal planning
- grocery shopping
- making time for friends and family
- getting a decent night's sleep
- exercising
- taking care of kids

Now imagine how you would get by if your day was even further complicated by the need to:

- do multiple nebulizer treatments every morning (takes over 2 hours at times)
- sort and fill pill boxes with 20-30+ oral meds every week
- clean and disinfect nebulizer supplies multiple times a day
- Do more nebs every afternoon if needed
- Plan for re-ordering all the meds
- Call in the med orders to the pharmacy. Wait for doc to refill. Run low. Stress out.

- Find the money to pay for the medicines. ARE YOU KIDDING ME?
- Apply for copay assistance programs and foundation grant money to help cover the expenses
- Fight with insurance over prior authorization denials – DON'T GET ME STARTED!!
- Schedule follow up visits with endocrinology, pulmonology, nutrition, physical therapy, primary care, etc, etc...
- Do more nebulizer treatments every evening.
- Administer IV antibiotics 3 or 4 times daily for 2-4 weeks at a time
- Don't forget to separate that oral antibiotic from this vitamin or that dairy product!
- Have labs drawn regularly
- Check blood sugars, administer insulin if necessary, Count your carbs
- Eat even when you don't feel hungry, just to keep your weight up
- Manage feeding tube and supplements

That to-do list just barely scratches the surface of what life is like for most patients fighting Cystic Fibrosis. The illness might also pile on complications such as *insomnia, headaches, joint pain, infertility, chest pain, Allergic Bronchopulmonary Aspergillosis (ABPA), Non-Tuberculous Mycobacterium, Lung Transplant,* and *Liver Transplant,* and the list goes on and on. The conversations CF patients and parents of children with CF are forced to have are certainly not for the faint of heart. A person with CF must also take a myriad of different medications daily. Here is just a sampling:

MED NAME	Dosing Instructions
CF Multivitamin	Take 1 cap by mouth twice daily with food
Vitamin D3	One cap by mouth once daily
Vitamin K	1 tab by mouth twice daily
Vitamin A	1 cap by mouth once daily
Vitamin E	1 cap by mouth once daily
Pancreatic Enzymes	5 caps by mouth with every meal and 3 caps with every snack
Albuterol inhaler	Inhale 2 puffs twice daily and every 4-6 hours as needed for shortness of breath
Pulmozyme	Take via nebulizer twice daily
Hypertonic Saline	Take via nebulizer twice daily
Ursodiol	2 caps by mouth twice daily
Azithromycin	By mouth once daily
CFTR modulator	By mouth twice daily
Inhaled antibiotic #1	Used via nebulizer every day, 2 or 3 times daily depending on the antibiotic. Sometimes held during IV antibiotic courses for exacerbation
Inhaled antibiotic #2	Used via nebulizer every day, 2 or 3 times daily depending on the antibiotic. Sometimes held during IV antibiotic courses for exacerbation
Short acting Insulin	With all meals and snacks containing carbs
Long acting insulin	Daily for basal blood sugar control
Anti-anxiety/Anti-depressant	By mouth once daily
Vest or percussor	Twice daily
Antibiotics for ABPA	Two to three times daily via nebulizer or Orally twice daily
IV antibiotic #1	Through IV twice daily, infused over 1 hour for 2-3 weeks during CF exacerbation
IV antibiotic #2	Through IV every 8 hours, infused over 4 hours for 2-3 weeks during CF exacerbation

IV antibiotic #3	Through IV every 8 hours, infused over 30 minutes for 2-3 weeks during CF exacerbation
Oral antibiotic	May be added if IVs don't cover all the bacteria growing in the lungs for 2-3 weeks during CF exacerbation
Port flushes and dressing changes	Frequency depends on whether the patient is on IV's at the time

But there is hope for patients with CF. The advancements made in the last several decades have extended the life expectancy of CF patients from the teens into the mid-to-late 40's! Amazing medications are now on the market that treat the underlying cause of CF and will hopefully prevent young children with CF from ever developing severe lung disease. It was truly miraculous to witness the improvements in patients whose genetics qualified them for these drugs. But there is still a lot of research to be done to ensure that every CF patient has access to one of these medications. The cure for CF is yet to be discovered, but the advent of new medications to help prevent further decline has brought us that much closer and there is so much hope.

As a CF pharmacist for nearly 10 years, I witnessed my patients' harrowing fight firsthand. They fight with everything they have simply to be present and get through each day. One day at a time. I am privileged I was able to be part of their lives, including Jen's, and will always consider them to be among the most inspiring, brave, and resilient people I will ever know.

• Thirteen •

Short and Sweet

Various Authors

The quality of life is about finding a happy balance between work, family, and friends. They are the very foundation of our lives. Some of our friends and family are succinct and to the point. What they have to say is still so important, still worth mentioning. This chapter is from friends and family who just wanted to keep it short and sweet.

Sally Ellis, her stepmother

I first met Jen just before she turned 4 years old – in the church parking lot where her brother was getting baptized. I stood there, and she put her arms out to me. Of course, I took her in my arms. Duane, her dad, was shocked and told me, "she doesn't do that." For me, I think I fell in love with her at that moment. She began to call me her Sonora mom, and she was the child of my heart.

Watching her in her swimming lessons, I remember the day when she finally dove off the side of the pool. She was so flexible, and I loved watching her do gymnastics. As she older, we could see her grow into a beautiful young woman, and always with such a kind heart. But she developed a backbone. When she was younger, we worried that she would allow people to walk all over her. But we watched her growth here too. She was agreeable and pretty easy going, but she had her "line in the sand." She reminded me a lot of dad in this area.

She was comfortable in her skin. I remember when we traveled to Santa Barbara for her great aunt Mary's birthday celebration. Her grandpa Otto and her aunt Georgia were with us too. She came out in her jeans, Doc Marten boots, and plaid shirt. She was "ready to go." She knew what she wanted... even when it came to unique presents: a bow for 8th-grade graduation, a Kimber 1911 handgun for college graduation, and a Golden Boy shotgun for her 40th birthday.

Her religious beliefs and spirituality were such an important part of her being. She never pushed her religion on someone, but she was always happy to share with anyone. Words that come to my mind when thinking of Jen: grace, beauty, sensitivity, strength, caring, and smiling.

To the end, I will share the words I spoke at the service for Ally, Jen's beloved niece, "So let me say before we part, so much of me is made of what I learned from you. You'll be with me, like a handprint on my heart. No matter how our stories end, I know you have rewritten mine. I do believe I have been changed for the better. And because I knew you, I have been changed for good" (from Wicked). Thank you, Jen.

Danielle Evans, a friend

She is more precious than words. She is a treasure more precious than gold. Her faith and love for our Jesus was pure joy! She lived and loved. She was a wonderful, super Wonder Woman who puts others first and a shining light for my walk with our Lord.

Leo Gonzalez, a friend and former co-worker

Jen was my friend. I remember she would walk into a room and light it up. She was the kind of person people wanted to be around. Working for her was a blast, but after work was better. I knew she had medical problems, but it never stopped her. She was a strong woman. My friend was tough, there were some days her body was hurting her, but she pushed on. My friend was brave. I love talking to her about everything; we would eat, drink, good times. Jen was a kind person; she is what this world needs more of; she was my friend. I used to call her baby sister. I was considered family. I love the way she laughed and then snorted, which only made you love her more. I remember her smile and her these eyes, beautiful. She was as smart as she was beautiful. I know her body was tired, but she had a strong soul. She always made you feel important; that was her way. And someday, she would be kooky, which only made you love her more. She was a blessing in my life, and I thank God for that. Jen was my friend. I know she is in heaven, waiting for us to be with her again. Jen holds a spot for me at that table. We need to catch up. I miss you every day. I love you, baby sister. Until that time.

Loretta Jensen, a friend

I met Jen as we both volunteered at The Union Gospel Mission in Coeur d'Alene. Our time there grew into a friendship, a sister-ship, that I will always, always treasure. Jen and I had much in common, and we clicked instantly. While Jen was excellent at handling conflict, her radiant smile lit up any room when the time called for it. Jesus' light shone brightly through Jen. And what a blast she was to be around!! Her sense of adventure was great; whether we were shooting at the range or cruising in her Mini with the top down, Jen was so joy-filled. I remember when she and Amanda Morgan came to visit me in the hospital, and the thing with Jen was, no matter where we were, you could always count on lots of laughter. Lots. Times with Jen were the best.

Jen was definitely small and spunky with a fight in her, and she was also an encourager. At UGM, she did so well at capturing the attention of others when it came time to teach and pray. Her personality and wisdom created a safe environment inviting others to share openly. Jen showed me some of my blind spots in life, but it wasn't to tell me what I was doing wrong, to fix me. Jen was there, showing me what I was doing right and cheering me on. She gave me the courage to push through the hard stuff. She saw my abilities and strengths when I did not. If I was overwhelmed, Jen spoke truth to my identity. She brought me the courage to fight harder.

Not only did Jen encourage others, but she was also courageous. Jen had many other Christ-like qualities, as well. She had a confidence that mirrored her readiness and made one feel secure. She was focused, a good listener, discerning and tender-hearted, and always looking for a good laugh. Jen is someone I will always greatly admire. Until we meet again in combat boots...

Phouthakone Milaythong (Ting), a friend

Jennifer Ellis, aka Jennifer McKenna, where do I begin? I met Jennifer at Foothill high school in 1991. In my freshman year, I had three classes with her, and our first class was Physical Education (PE). She made our PE class together fun. There was something about Jen when she smiled. It is so infectious that you have to smile along with her. What is not to like about Jennifer? She was the kindest person you meet and genuine. Her laugh was the best. OMG, if she laughed so hard, she started to "hack up a cough aka hack up a lung," and you tend to laugh with her regardless of the situation. I cherished all my time with Jennifer all four years of high school and beyond. We lost contact for a couple of years, and Facebook reunited us in 2010. It had been over 12 years, and a lot had happened. I found out she was married to her soulmate and finally got her dream car, a "Mini Cooper." Over the year, we kept in contact with each other.

I finally went back to Bakersfield to spend a day with Jennifer and meet Corey for the first time. We had a blast. What I remember and stuck out the most was, she carried a gun into Subway! Subway in Bakersfield. As we parked, I popped my trunk and asked Jennifer if she wanted to keep her Kimber; she said, "It is okay, I can carry it inside." I was like, hmm, okay, it must be Bakersfield. We had lunch, and she took me to her place of work, Second Amendment Sports, and we had a blast shooting Zombies.

After looking back, it is not how often you see someone, but how we can connect with them, and our bond never changed. I cherished every moment when I talked, messaged, or saw Jennifer because she was a fantastic person inside and out. She taught me never to give up, always have hope regardless of any situation, and believe in God.

"Good friends are like stars. You don't always see them, but you know they're always there" - Unknown

Georgia Stewart, her aunt

Jen is my sweet niece. I didn't get to be around her very much as she was growing up. It seems time and distance were in the way, even as she got older. However, the times we did have were full of love and concern for the ones she loved most.

Our common denominator was thicker than blood. We shared Jesus. I was so blessed that she would ask me to be part of her team in North Carolina at Chapel Hill.

One of the significant meetings we had was at her brother's wedding. I sat at the same table with Jen and her future husband, Corey. I could see that this was a good match. Jen was so brave, we all know this, but to see her so beautiful on her wedding day in 10 below zero weather, exaggeration, without a jacket, I knew she was truly tough.

Jennifer has left a "trail of Jesus" behind her. What a legacy. She has touched so many lives, so natural, so quirky, so herself.

I never knew her to put on airs for anyone. She was always "What you see is what you get." Our Aunt Mary Stewart had a 70th birthday party in Santa Barbara, CA. Everyone was dressed up, heels, jewelry, and nice dresses. The men wore sport coats. Not Jen! She was always true to herself, jeans, cotton shirt, and tennis shoes. So confident in who she was.

I remember watching her at a family reunion in Oklahoma, teaching Aunt Mary Jane how to shoot a gun. Yes, Jen was an official "gun packin' mama." 100 lbs. of don't mess with me. The times I've had with Jen have always been centered on one person, Jesus. We talked about relationships and love for our family.

Jesus was always the answer to any problem. When she and Corey moved to Idaho, I believe that's when she found her purpose in The Lord. I know she was a blessing to all she came in contact with. All I know is Jen was very special, and I love her very much. Because of our common denominator, Jesus, we will see each other again one day. Anyone who knew her knew her big heart and love for God. Her chains are gone, and she is now free. I love you, Jen.

Abby Taylor, Home Health Nurse (who has a husband with CF)

I had the privilege of caring for Jen during what I would call an incredibly tough 1-2 years of her life. I genuinely don't believe that she looked at that time as incredibly tough but as a gift of time. What drew me into Jen was her contagious personality. She was so positive and at peace, no matter what the outcome would be. Most importantly, she knew Jesus and knew no matter how long her life would be someday she would be with Him. This gave her a peace that was felt when I would visit, and she could barely catch her breath just sitting on her couch where she lived most of her last year of life. While I'm sure she may have wanted her circumstances to change, she wasn't fearful if they didn't.

When I reflect on her life, I'm reminded of the scripture in 1 Corinthians 5:55 that says, "oh death, where is your sting." Jen knew she would be with Jesus someday. Knowing and believing this broke the power of the fear of death in her life. She was able to live with great hope of a better day when she would no longer struggle to breathe.

What we can learn from Jen: One day, we will all face death. It is important to consider now what you want to give your life to. Too many go through life without purpose and end up with regret when they get to the end. Jen realized that believing in Jesus meant the promise of heaven when she died. Therefore, she didn't have to see death as something to be afraid of. Each of us should consider what we believe about God now and live out that belief while we can.

On a lighter side, I remember coming to her house 3-4 weeks in a row, and every day there were more people at her home. I joked with her that she would probably have a huge party there the next time I came over. Well, sure enough, her iv line went bad during her surprise 40th birthday party. I showed up, and Fire Pizza oven was parked in her driveway. I just laughed with her, thinking she could never top this many people when I visit next. She kept a smile the whole visit, even though I had to poke her multiple times because of her poor vein status. What we can learn from this: "Consider it pure joy when you face trials of many kinds because you know that the testing of your faith develops perseverance" (James 1:2-3). Jen would constantly be joyful in times when circumstances were trying. This was made possible because of her faith in God. I'm so thankful for the precious times I got to spend with Jen. I loved hearing about the next race Corey would be running or meeting her new puppy Samson. I had the privilege of meeting her parents and friends. What a beautiful tribe of people she had surrounded her life with. She loved her tribe deeply.

What we can learn from Jen: you become more like those with whom you hang around. Fill your life with a tribe of people that encourages, strengthens, and challenges you to become the person you were created to be.

Kelly Watson, transplant coordinator at UNC Hospital:

So, I am a coordinator. Not the party planning kind, but a medical one. In my case, the lung transplant kind. In my job, I meet all sorts of people from all walks of life, different shapes, ages, races, religions. However, they are all sharing one thing; they're dying. Jen was too.

I remember when her referral came through. It read something like this...41-year-old female with Cystic Fibrosis, 4L oxygen requirement, drug-resistant bacteria. Her story read like many others; only this one also came with a list of centers that had turned her down. The following day I get a call from her pharmacist, which turned out to be the first of many "firsts."

Lindsey, her pharmacist, called to advocate for Jen. I called to make sure that I could see how much more Jen is than just what is on paper. To offer me her number and any assistance she could provide. She wasn't sure how or what I may need but wanted me to know that whatever I needed, Jen and her posse would make it happen. I had a feeling then that I would like Jen. I didn't realize how much.

Our process is challenging. As a transplant team, we have a difficult job. From a medical standpoint, we review cases and evaluate each candidate's chance at success. I know this sounds terrible, but we have so many more people who need transplants than organs available to give them one. A lung transplant requires the loss of life to provide a chance at life. There are no living donors, no dialysis, no other options, only the loss of life. This exchange is a very delicate balance, so we as a transplant team have to look at more than people just wanting a transplant. We have to look at the chances of survival, willingness to go the extra mile, caregiver support, comorbidities, fitness level, overall health. I mean, there are more factors in this decision than you can imagine.

On a Tuesday morning in December, we sat down as a multidisciplinary team to discuss the case that is Jen McKenna. We recognized that she was complex, to say the least. We reviewed her records, looked at her medications, her rate of decline, her oxygen requirement, and the resistant bacteria that had made Jen so sick. Our immunocompromised infectious disease (ICID) doctor felt that there might be some options; however, he needed more data.

My first call to Jen was the first time a transplant center had not outright turned her down, the first time a team seemed interested. So, our first call was tears and excitement followed by a sobering statement when I had to tell Jen, "I cannot make any promises, we need to look at some of your cultures, and we need a sample sent to a research lab." After what felt like forever, including lab tests and cultures, the ICID physician told the team that he thought we had an effective antibiotic plan. However, she would be an increased risk patient, period. Was she a patient with the grit, the family, the commitment, and drive to fight the fight? Without hesitation, I assured the team she did. I shared the conversation I had with her pharmacist. I shared her commitment, and I told them she was willing to move across the country with her mother to meet whatever criteria we set forth. The multidisciplinary decision was that we invite her to come for an initial consult, NO promises, but an appointment to discuss if we could do more.

I left this meeting excited about sharing this news with Jen. This is the call you look forward to making. It's the call that delivers a glimmer of hope. I dial up Jen's cell, and she answers right away; little to my knowledge, I am on speakerphone. I tell Jen the team wants to meet her, I tell her I still cannot make promises and that this only the first natural step, I hear her start to cry, then I hear cheers and more tears, and Jen says, "oh, Kelly, you're on speaker, I am at my doctor's appt., Corey is here, my pharmacist is here and so is my doctor." Best. Day. Ever.

· Fourteen ·

In Her Own Words...

Jen McKenna

"Iron sharpens iron. So one man sharpens another" (Proverbs 27:17).

We look to others to be motivated, to be stimulated, and to be energized. We bring people into our lives to drive us to be better and to live our lives to the fullest. It is no wonder people gravitated towards Jen. This energy she had is what sharpened us to become who we are, to be better versions of ourselves. It reflected the fullness of life: physical, emotional, social, as well as spiritual. It meant to be joined together and grow to meet the challenges in life and even ready for eternal life, through faith in Jesus Christ. Strength and courage surrounded her every day and we all learned to laugh along with her.

Jen was passionate about many things in life. She loved her life, loved her friends, loved God, loved her husband, and loved her family. Here are some great, insightful things... in her own words.

- I love cheese, especially after eating ice cream. You know – a cheese chaser.
- I had fried spam and scrambled eggs for breakfast this morning. Toast with Brummel and Brown "butter" and a thin layer of olallieberry jam. And orange juice. My beautiful husband made it for me, no questions asked.
- I constantly daydream.
- I like to wear makeup, but I hate washing my face at night. Not a good practice!
- I work very hard at work, and when I get home, I am very lazy.
- I believe that we have all made mistakes and we have all done some really big bad or stupid things. It's inevitable, because we are human. We have full control on whether we lie about it, when the matter comes up. The only thing a decent person can do about it is be truthful. I despise lying.
- My Kimber 1911 is bigger than I am. Sometimes I am too weak to rack the slide.
- If I could live in another setting, I'd be a cowgirl in the old west!
- When Moses threw the 10 Commandments down and broke them, was he the first to "break the law?"
- If you could rub two big lizards together, I bet it would sound a lot like me putting lotion on my poor, dry, neglected hands!!!

- The newest book series I am enjoying IMMENSELY is the Janet Evanovich novels about Stephanie Plum, the bounty hunter. I want to be a bounty hunter.

- I fear the germs and viruses of prison. Did you know that you don't even have your own underwear!!? A laundry cart rolls by, and you pick a set of undies and sports bra out of the cart. There is a HUGE possibility that those heavily bleached undergarments were worn by a diseased hooker the day before. (I shudder as I type this) At least, this is what I saw in a tour of the county jail up north.

- I used to drive a purple pick-up truck and his name was Grimace.

- I love small dinners and get togethers. Large gatherings are nerve wracking. I love God and bible teaching and intimate settings, but I have great anxiety sitting in a sanctuary.

- I like rock climbing with my honey, but I'm afraid of heights.

- "It's easy to be a warrior, when I have the best army supporting me! ". I told one of infusion nurses this, today. We have so many friends and family supporting our family in labor, prayer, and love... near and far! I couldn't possibly "tag" all of you. But we can name each one of you and how you have supported us so far. We thank God for you, we SEE you, and we treasure you

- With all these tubes fighting for nostril space, how am I gonna fit my finger up there, too!??!
- I am the unofficial record holder at work for being the biggest pig: I am 5'3" 124 lbs and can eat a 30oz steak with beans and a potato and a drink in one sitting. My friend who is 6'3 at a little over 200 can't finish it!
- Dude! Acme is a real word!! I thought it was just Wile E Coyote's favorite brand! (oh, and it means "highest point, summit)
- Next time you refer to a "buttload" of stuff, just know: it's a real unit of measurement! 1 butt = 2 hogsheads or 4 barrels or 126 gallons. Some people nowadays may grimace at this coarse-sounding language, but medieval villagers wouldn't bat an eye!
- Whenever I see "Juicy" across the seat of a girl's pants, I wanna get her some Imodium and about 10 ft of berth!!
- I watched "Shaft" for the first time. The 1971 film. Awesome. I now want to end all my imperative sentences with "baby" or "sugar!"
- Technically, Moses was the first person with a tablet downloading data from the cloud.
- Hi friends!! Big news that some have heard and some haven't, but I don't really know how to present. So, I'm gonna paste a post did last week: "My awesome wife is the true Ironman of the family. I may be able to compete for 18+ hours and train for 6 months

non-stop. But this woman endures physical and mental toughness day after day after day. She is the Iron-woman. As of late, we get to visit the Univ of North Carolina in late December about getting on the lung transplant list. When I thought extreme triathlon was life-changing... Praise God... this is beyond life-changing. Thank you to everyone for all the support and prayer. This is pretty exciting." I love my husband.

- When I yell at the dog to stop barking, I wonder if he's like "this is awesome! We're barking together!"

- What are some good descriptions for how you feel, when you're sick? I find that "good," "better," and "tired" are my typicals, but they really don't inform people? Like... "I am tired, but I could play a low-concentration game like Yahtzee.". I like that. I think "hammered shit" is hilarious and descriptive, but to me that sounds more like a collision than being sick.

- One of my goals in life is to be a more compassionate and loving person. I think it will make my sanctuary-sitting experiences much better.

- My dear husband. It's funny... growing up, when I thought about love, I would try to picture the face of the man that I would one day love and marry. I often wondered what he would look like, and how I would recognize him. Sometimes I even wished that God would put a big red arrow pointing down at "the one," so that I didn't have to blunder through dating, and I could just beeline for the guy with the red arrow. Well, you know, and I know that it just doesn't happen that way. Even worse, I couldn't really picture marriage, because I had not fallen in love with the man that God intended for me. Now, though, having the pleasure of knowing you, watching you, being your best friend, and your wife, I look at your face and you radiate love. I see your love applied in countless ways. God has blessed me beyond my wildest dreams. I am so thankful, every minute, every hour of every day that you are my permanent Valentine!

This was Jen's last social media post to everyone prior to her surgery on May 22, 2019 (from Facebook on May 14):

Hello! So, I have been in the hospital for almost two weeks. I had an exacerbation of existing infections kind of gang up on me. Usually, what that looks like is I breathe nonstop – not quite a pant, but I don't rest between breaths. I also cough more and have to increase my oxygen flow. My doctors got all that under control really fast, like they really what they're doing!

At this time, we have determined that I just don't have enough margin in my health, to be discharged to go to our temporary home. I am staying in the hospital until my new lungs come in. The good news is my lung allocation score got updated, in light of my exacerbation, and I am at the top of the list for our area. My score gets updated this Thursday, again, and it will likely drop, but it reflects my improved state. I can't really complain. But I hope a good match comes available by then. I can handle that.

In the meantime, I am working harder than ever to gain weight and strength. When I look at my exercise, it's less strenuous that it was a week before I was admitted. But whether it's the hard-hitting meds, slight decline in health, or sitting in a hospital room, exercise is harder. So is eating. I space out exercise from eating, because my lungs start feeling insufficient from either activity. To complicate the situation, I have lost my appetite, and need to eat small but frequent snacks. I need to gain weight, so that my body can sustain itself, as it heals from surgery. Bacteria loves to get into sutures and start multiplying and there may be remnants of my NTM lingering in my sinuses and trachea. We don't want those infecting my new lungs. So, eating takes priority over working out.

This is the hardest hospital stay I have ever done. But I have some great things to be thankful for! Awesome staff, nice accommodations, a stationary bike in my room, my husband, and my mom is here is with me. With the IV pumps, oxygen line, and monitor leads, every simple task is more like a procedure. She helps with a lot of the extra steps, and it all adds up to a better rest. Having mom is also invaluable in reducing anxiety. And my dad and stepmom are coming to visit. They'll give mom a break.

Today was a challenging day for me, and I received an influx of encouraging texts and scriptures from friends. They refocused me on God's greatness. I am so comforted! Thank you for praying, thank you for letting God lead your heart!

• *Fifteen* •

The Beauty in Our Tears

Corey McKenna

"Today is the day the Lord has made; let us be glad and rejoice in it" (Psalm 118:24). This passage from the author of Psalms was something Jen lived by each day, no matter how challenging things were in life. Today is the day the Lord has made. 2019 started amazing, knowing we were headed to North Carolina for a lung transplant. Leading up to May 23, I was completely optimistic about the outcome. Little did I know I would not be coming home with my wife. I left North Carolina with her ashes in a box. She was called home to our Lord and what started as excitement ended in tragedy. I was devastated beyond any words, any feelings, any thoughts. My entire life was just flipped upside down and sent sideways. I was now alone without my partner, my wife, my love, my best friend. How do I go on and move forward? Many a night early on, I sobbed uncontrollably, in the dark. It would hit at the oddest parts of the day. I did not know what I was going to do.

People were kind and supportive of my grief, asking how I was doing. I think I put on a good poker face. I would tell people I am doing okay when in fact, I probably was not. As days and nights went on, the one thing I did not expect to experience was *silence*. No more coughing. No more oxygen machine. No more nebulizer machine. No more laughter. It was too quiet, too still in the house. Samson, our Bernese Mountain dog, was confused. He could smell mom's clothes, but mom was not there. I know he was asking, "when is mom coming home?" I did not know what to tell him; so, I just hugged him. He would sit in her spot on the couch, with his favorite toy, waiting. He knew she was not coming home.

In August, we held *A Celebration of Life* service to ensure everyone who could attend did. We were so grateful for those who made the journey to Coeur d'Alene. We held a smaller graveside service for family and close friends and much larger church service for anyone. It was beautiful to see everyone and celebrate Jen's life and, of course, mourn her loss. We all laughed, cried, hugged, cried some more, and laughed some more. It could not have been any better. One thing I shared with people was this poem:

If I could trade tomorrow for yesterday with you,
I'd close my eyes and pray for night to come.
If tears could build a stairway and heartache build a lane,
I'd take you by the hand and lead you home.
I think of you in silence, so often speak your name,
A million tears at least I must have cried.

Your leaving brought such sorrow, it broke my heart in two,
A million times at least I've asked God why.
But though I'm left to wonder why you had to leave so soon,
When there were still at least a million
Little things we'd planned to do...
In my heart I know that you are in His loving care,
And I know the day will come we'll meet again.
So, I'll just keep loving you,
I'll hold you in my heart.
And I think of you with
Every breath I take.
Until then my sweet love...

After it was all done, people went back to their normal lives, but I was left with an empty house. Silence crept through and it did not seem to get better. I competed in two local triathlons in August and traveled to Orcas Island, WA, for Swimrun in late September. Those events seemed to provide a bit of normalcy in my life. It did not seem enough though, but it was okay.

There were so many *firsts* that happened in the Fall. Halloween was a big deal in our neighborhood. I chose not to do anything about it. My first Thanksgiving without her happened. Her first birthday without her happened a few days later. Neither were very easy. Then, it was my first Christmas without her and the worst − our anniversary on January 1st. One step at a time, I found the inner strength to make it through each of these *firsts*. God gave me the strength, and I know He came along to help through it. He longed to help me through it. He did not want me to suffer. The very thing — suffering — that made me wonder if God is cruel. The very thing that made me question God's goodness. The very thing I could not understand in Jen's passing. The very thing I did not want in God's plan ever, ever, ever. Not for me. Not anyone. Ever. But God did not want me to suffer. He does allow it in doses to increase our trust in Him that He knows what He is doing.

In late October, it was the first time in over four months that I had not cried at least once during the day. I call that progress. I was fortunate to be asked by Terry Gurno to speak at the first *Day of Influence* in January 2020. Like TED Talk, I was one of eight influential speakers who told their story, whatever it was. Writing and practicing my talk over the few months leading up to the day was very therapeutic and healing. By the time I gave my talk in early January, I was in a much better space and place than the previous several months. Again, progress.

While not what any of us imagined in 2019, I am quite thankful Jen was not having to endure this in 2020 while COVID was happening. I imagine none of us would have been allowed in the hospital or, if we were, would not be allowed to leave. I shudder to think of Jen being alone through it — going through the operation alone or, worse, potentially dying alone. But then I remember God's plan is perfect, and He knew what He was doing all along. She did not have to go through this alone. Family and friends were able to be part of it, in some way, however large or small. One noted loss in 2020 was the unexpected passing of Galen Norsworthy, the author of Chapter 5 in this book. He went to sleep one day and did not wake up. His death was tragic and devasting to all his family and friends. I know he and Jen, along with Steve Williams (Jen's mom's husband who passed away in February 2019), are in heaven, laughing it up and trading stories while watching down on us from above.

In the end, my catastrophic loss taught me the incredible power of choice — to enter the darkness of grief and feel sorrow, as I did after her death. It was to express the calmness and peace within me, even as I continued to work, care for people, and even fall in love again. I wanted to gain as much as I could from the loss without neglecting ordinary responsibilities. I had had enough of the constant tears, and I did not want to respond to the tragedy in a way that would exacerbate the internal chaos I already experienced.

This experience taught me that loss reduces people to a state of almost total brokenness and vulnerability. Grieving takes time. For some, it takes a bit longer. Eventually, I needed to become a contributing member of the community, willing to receive love again. That decision was not easy to make at first. It probably never is. Naturally, people feel cautious about loving again because they are afraid of losing again. Is it even possible to love after loss? It is a choice I get to make, to go down that road, and risk the possibility of loss again.

It takes tremendous strength and courage to love when you are broken. Brokenness forces us to find a source of love outside ourselves. I was not impressed with the online dating scene and felt like it was a huge waste of time and money.

Then, one day in late February, a local female triathlete was looking for a place to rent. Knowing she was in a dead-end relationship, it sounded like she was moving out. I reached out and asked if she was interested in getting a beer. On March 11th, 2020, I met Katy Beck at one of our town's local pubs, Daft Badger. We talked for more than two hours. After we left, we both knew our lives had changed. A week later, COVID shut everything down and forced us to hang out and get to know each other. Surprisingly, COVID was the best thing to happen to us. Days turned into weeks which turned into months. We spent the summer weekends riding bikes, playing Scrabble, watching movies, just hanging out. We just found love in each other and at the perfect time in our lives. After several months, we started talking about marriage, and on December 4th, 2020, in Leavenworth, WA, I asked her to marry me. We cannot wait to see what the Lord will do for us as we plan to get married in 2022. We knew He brought us together for all the right reasons and at the right time. Today is the day the Lord has made...

As with every fallen leaf on the breeze, Jen left a big huge hole in this world when she passed, but the impressions she left on all of us will last forever. She was welcomed into Heaven by God and by those who died before her, and she, in turn, received close friends who passed after. While each passing moment is one step forward, those passing moments give me the memory of my late wife – the huge smile, the snort-laugh, the genuine nature of her calm disposition, and I think, most importantly, the reliance on God through all of it. Through her, I am reminded of her strength and courage as she endured some of the most challenging and most difficult things I think any of us could ever imagine. She knew God was with her wherever she went.

We will all experience grief in some way, in many ways, in our lives. Grief never ends, but it changes. It is a passage in life, but not a place to stay. Grief is not a sign of weakness either, or a lack of faith. It is merely the price of love. Finding the inner strength is what helps each of us achieve whatever we need to cope and move forward. Anything is possible, nothing is impossible, or whatever saying you use, having the push to move forward is what allows us to grab hold of that inner strength.

We are all given the strength to remember that life is so very fragile. We are all vulnerable. And we will all, at some point in our lives, fall. We will all fall. We will all have a tragedy that will cause us to fall, but we must get back up. We must carry this in our hearts, that what we have is special, that it can be taken from us, and that will be tested. We will be tested to our very souls, all of us. It is these times; it is this pain that allows us to look inside ourselves. The pain we experience will let us grow closer to God and closer to others.

Not a day passes that I do not miss her, knowing one day we will see each other again in heaven. I also know she is no longer suffering and can breathe fully without complications. I know she is there with friends and family members who passed before her. And, in some way, I think she permitted me to let go, allowed me to move forward, to find myself, and to fall in love again. I know she sacrificed everything, never gave up hope or trust in God. For now, moving forward with strength and courage, knowing today is the day the Lord has made, I love and celebrate her for what she left for me on this earth and celebrate it with those closest to me.

Epilogue

Stoic Determination

So much has happened since Jen passed away – the death of mutual friends, grief, healing, more grief, racial tensions in North Carolina, COVID, more healing, love, 17-year cicadas in North Carolina, and even a massive dust storm from the Sahara Desert blew across the Atlantic and hit North Carolina. I cannot help but wonder how things might have turned out if Jen did not pass away. Transplant surgeries are an intense process. There are so many little things that many of us would not even think or imagine. Double lung transplant recipients require intense therapy – teaching a person to walk again, to breathe again, to function normally again. Life itself would change: new eating habits, constant cleanliness to avoid infection, endless post-transplant medications, and multiple trips back and forth to the hospital for therapy and checkup appointments. The list was endless, almost dizzying.

Our bodies are such interesting machines. When a new pair of lungs are put inside someone, the body does not recognize it even though there were a pair of lungs in its place earlier. A person's body undergoes a metamorphosis of sorts when it tries to accept a new organ. The body's natural response is to fit it off because it does not belong. Learning to breathe again was interesting as well. Just prior to surgery, the patient was breathing (even though it was difficult). Post-surgery forces the patient to learn how to breathe again. The patient must go through occupational therapy to learn how to walk again, to take a shower, to put on clothes and shoes, or how to handle utensils. Who knew? I think Jen would have jumped in with both feet and worked really hard at making it work.

I think there are times where we have to dig deep to do what it takes to get the job done. I think of my long course triathlon experiences, realizing I have been up since 2am, shoveling down food to get ready for an event, traveling to the start, setting up the equipment, all before I actually start. Then, however long it takes, sometimes 17 hours or more, I come off the high of finishing such a challenging event. Again, the body is an amazing machine. It goes through all of this work with little to no rest until the athlete actually goes to sleep some 20+ hours later. I think it is sense of stoic determination, finding out what we are capable of doing when our bodies are put to the extreme test.

For a person who lives a *normal, healthy* life (if we can call it that), walking across the room, taking a shower, getting to the car, washing dishes, or any other everyday activity, these things are not overly difficult or challenging. For a person who has cystic fibrosis and decreased lung capacity, it can be extremely difficult, sometimes almost impossible. They give every ounce of energy to get to the finish, even if the finish line was walking

50 feet to get a drink of water in the kitchen. It too was stoic determination.

No question Jen would have dug deep to get the job done. She worked hard prior to the transplant so I was confident she would work hard after it. She would have dug deep to get the job done in therapy, learning how to walk, putting on clothes, tying her shoes, brushing her teeth. She would have endured the challenge of walking 50 feet, then 100 feet, then down the hall, then outside. Heck, I think she would have endured the COVID nonsense that paralyzed the world in 2020. Determination and persistence.

As I continue to find the joys amid the loss, I cannot help but think how different things would be if Jen was still alive. No question it would be really hard to get through each day. I would still have work and we both would have to adjust to a new way of living. Each passing day would make us stronger. It would be tough at first, but I think it would get easier over time. Support from others would have been key to success. No matter where we are in life, we are all surrounded by amazing support systems in friends and family. They jump to at the drop of a hat. They come to our aid when we have fallen. They comfort us in time of need. COVID would have made it much more difficult though. People may not have been allowed in the house because of the high risk of infection. Jokingly but somewhat serious is that people may have had to wear hazmat suits to enter the house.

The grief felt over the last couple of years is both bitter and sweet. I still feel sorrow, there's no question about that, but I also have immense joy in my heart. Each day brings excitement and happiness. The pain in my heart is still immense, but the simple pleasures of life have changed my perspectives because of where I am in life. Oddly, I do not put with people's nonsense any longer. I find it truly extraordinary. I have been broken; yet never I have been so whole. I thank God for that. I thank all the families for that. I thank Katy for that. And, in a way, I thank Jen for that. I am content, strong, and at peace.

As a final thought, I was trying to figure out how to bring this to a close. I could write more and more, but as I tell my doctorate students, "you have to find a place to just stop writing." While it is not the end of the story, it is merely a transition. Trying to figure the best way to wrap up, I was reminded of Jen's *Celebration of* Life service in August 2019. I chose the song *No Longer Slaves* to be sung by Zach and Lauren Penston at her service (they crushed it, by the way). It truly captures what we believe and who we are in life:

You unravel me
With a melody
You surround me with a song
Of deliverance
From my enemies
'Til all my fears are gone
I am no longer a slave to fear
I am a child of God

From my mother's womb
You have chosen me
Love has called my name
I've been born again to a family
Your blood flows through my veins
I'm no longer a slave to fear
I am a child of God.

I am surrounded
By songs of deliverance
We've been liberated
From our bondage
We're the sons and the daughters
Let us sing our freedom

You split the sea
So, I could walk right through it
My fears are drowned in perfect love
You rescued m
So, I could stand and say
I am a child of God
I am a child of God
Yes, I am a child of God.

Acknowledgements

I want to thank all those who played a role in her life's journey, however large or small. Your support, love, encouragement, prayers, and energy helped us overcome so much. I love each and every person and am so thankful for your contributions:

Virginia (and Steve) Williams

Duane and Sally Ellis

Joe, Nikki, and Josie (and Ally) Ellis

Michael and Jeanette McKenna

Otto Ellis

Jean Wilhite

Georgia Stewart

Josh and Katie Lewis

Joe and Holly Raymond

Galen and Lita Norsworthy

Kurt, Sara and Aaron Staeuble

Zach and Lauren Penston

Matt and Dana Janes

Keith and Becky Foster

Mike and Jackie Maker

Bill and Jan Vetter

Amanda Morgan

Robin Olson

Katy Beck
Perry and Anita Safron
Church Family at Coeur d'Alene Bible Church
All Heart Infusion
Union Gospel Mission
Dr. Jeffrey Hananell and his CF team
Dr. Michael McCarthy and his CF team
The University of North Carolina transplant hospital team

And the countless others of whom I may have forgotten

· Contact ·

Thank you for reading this book. Our prayer for everyone is to be inspired by how to live life to the fullest. We are blessed in this life and we need to make the most of it. We are excited at what the future holds for each of us.

If you are interested in reaching out to any of us, feel free to contact me and I will be happy to forward any correspondence to any of the authors in this book.

Corey McKenna
corey_mckenna@yahoo.com

CPSIA information can be obtained
at www.ICGtesting.com
Printed in the USA
BVHW041619050721
611164BV00016BA/706